Teaching

Second Edition

Dawn A. Oler, M.S., M.Ed., NBCT
Invitation to Teach Coordinator
Family and Consumer Sciences
Hinsdale Central High School
Hinsdale, Illinois

Publisher
The Goodheart-Willcox Company, Inc.
Tinley Park, Illinois
www.g-w.com

Introduction

This Workbook is designed for use with the *Teaching* text. It will help you understand, remember, and apply facts and concepts about teaching presented in the text. It will also help you apply this learning to your future career goals.

The activities in this Workbook are divided into chapters that correspond to the chapters in the text. By reading the text first, you will have information you need to complete the activities. Try to complete the activities without referring to the text. If necessary, you can look at the book later to complete any questions you could not answer.

Many of the activities can be used as review guides when you study for tests and quizzes. Other activities, such as observations, rubrics, evaluations, and comparisons will ask for your opinions and ideas that cannot be judged as "right" or "wrong." These activities are designed to stimulate your thinking and help you apply information presented in the text.

The activities in this Workbook have been designed to increase your interest and understanding of the text material. The more thought you put into the activities, the more knowledge you will gain from them.

Cover image: Monkey Business Images/Shutterstock

Contents

Unit 3 The Learner

Unit 4 The Teacher

Chapter 10 What Makes an Effective Teacher?

Chapter 11 Planning for Instruction

Chapter 12 Instructional Methods

Chapter 13 Technology for Instruction

Chapter 14 The Role of Assessment

Chapter 15 Classroom Management

Chapter 16 The Next Steps to Becoming a Teacher

Chapter 1
Teaching as a Profession

Building Your Pedagogical Vocabulary

Activity A   **Name** _____   **Date** _____   **Period** _____

Part 1: Choose one or more important terms from this chapter. Do the following:

    A. Define the term(s)

    B. Provide an example of the word(s) in context

    C. Supply a visual representation of the term

You will have 15 minutes to complete this task and then present your term or terms to the class.

Part 2: While others are presenting, write their definitions, context that makes sense to you, and describe their visuals in the space provided.

Term	Definition	Context	Visual
Extracurricular activities			
Curriculum			
School-based curriculum			
Nonsectarian			
Paraprofessional			
Self-contained classroom			
Abstract thinking			

(Continued)

Term	Definition	Context	Visual
Collaborative learning			
Postsecondary education			
Technical schools			
Corporate trainers			
Curriculum developer			
Program director			
Developmental disabilities			
Parent educator			
Psychologist			
Diversity			
Advocate			
Salary schedule			
Portfolio			

Recognizing Effective Teaching

Activity B   Name _____ Date _____ Period _____

Complete each of the following items. Write your responses in the space provided.

Part 1: Brainstorm three qualities you have observed an effective teacher exhibit. Then give an example of how each quality played a positive role in your learning.

1. _____

   _____

2. _____

   _____

3. _____

   _____

Part 2: Partner with several other students, and compare and discuss your lists. Then individually write your answers to the questions that follow in the space provided.

4. What qualities do several of you have listed in common? _____

   _____

5. What makes these qualities important to teaching?

   _____

   _____

6. What is the perception of students when teachers exhibit these qualities?

   _____

   _____

7. How does that perception translate to student achievement?

   _____

   _____

Part 3: In a small team, create a skit that demonstrates two of the qualities you feel are most important for effective teachers to possess. Each person in your team must play a role with the *teaching quality* and *impact on student achievement* evident. Each team will have five minutes to perform its skit in front of the class. Use the following space to outline your skit.

   Optional: Video-record the skit to share with class.

   _____

   _____

   _____

   _____

   _____

   _____

There Is No "Typical" Day in Teaching, but...

During your day as a high school student you sit in a number of classes and engage with a variety of educators. To learn more about their roles as teachers, complete the following activities.

1. Arrange a *5–10 minute interview with three different educators* in your building. Interviews may take place during this class period (with teacher approval), lunch, during study hall, before or after school.

   The three educators I want to interview are:

   A. _____

   B. _____

   C. _____

2. E-mail the teachers and copy your teacher if asked to do so. Let the educators know you are considering the field of education as a career option and would value their honest insight and time.

3. On the following pages are five questions to ask each person you interview, you must come up with an additional three to five questions of your own, and get your teacher's approval of your questions prior to the interviews. Brainstorm your list questions in the space that follows and then include them on the following pages on which you will record their responses. You may want to personalize some of the questions to the teachers' position.

   A. _____
   _____

   B. _____
   _____

   C. _____
   _____

   D. _____
   _____

   E. _____
   _____

4. Provide the teachers with your questions ahead of time; confirm the interview date and time via e-mail or in person.

5. Record the teachers' responses on the following pages during your interviews.

6. Type up a one-page summary of the responses from each educator and a one page reflection on the interviews addressing the following questions. (maximum total of four pages) Attach your summary to this activity sheet for evaluation.

   A. What did you learn from the interviews?

   B. What responses surprised you? Why?

   C. What questions do you still have or arose as a result of these interviews?

   D. What other reflections do you have, if any, from the experience?

(Continued)

Name _____

Educator #1 Name: _____

Title: _____

Date of Interview: _____ **Time:** _____

Location: _____

1. What are the most important tasks you complete each day?_____

   _____

   _____

2. How do you make time to complete clerical tasks?

   _____

   _____

3. What factors determine what you teach (curriculum)? _____

   _____

   _____

4. What are some of the rewards of teaching? _____

   _____

   _____

5. What is the biggest challenge you face as a teacher? _____

   _____

   _____

6. _____?

   _____

   _____

7. _____?

   _____

   _____

8. _____?

   _____

   _____

9. _____?

   _____

   _____

10. _____?

   _____

   _____

(Continued)

Educator #2 Name: _____

Title: _____

Date of Interview: _____ **Time:** _____

Location: _____

1. What are the most important tasks you complete each day?

   _____

   _____

2. How do you make time to complete clerical tasks? _____

   _____

   _____

3. What factors determine what you teach (curriculum)? _____

   _____

   _____

4. What are some of the rewards of teaching? _____

   _____

   _____

5. What is the biggest challenge you face as a teacher? _____

   _____

   _____

6. _____?

   _____

   _____

7. _____?

   _____

   _____

8. _____?

   _____

   _____

9. _____?

   _____

   _____

10. _____?

   _____

   _____

(Continued)

Name _____

    Educator #3 Name: _____

    Title: _____

    Date of Interview: _____ **Time:** _____

    Location: _____

1. What are the most important tasks you complete each day? _____

    _____

    _____

2. How do you make time to complete clerical tasks? _____

    _____

    _____

3. What factors determine what you teach (curriculum)? _____

    _____

    _____

4. What are some of the rewards of teaching? _____

    _____

    _____

5. What is the biggest challenge you face as a teacher? _____

    _____

    _____

6. _____?

    _____

    _____

7. _____?

    _____

    _____

8. _____?

    _____

    _____

9. _____?

    _____

    _____

10. _____?

    _____

    _____

Career and Employment Options in the Field of Education

Teachers work in a variety of environments completing a range of professional responsibilities. The chart below lists the types of schools and other opportunities in education mentioned in the text. List examples for each within your own community and in your own words describe the key *features*.

Education Environment	Examples	Key Features
Preschool and Kindergarten Programs (E.C.E. Early Childhood Education)		
Elementary Schools		
Middle or Junior High Schools		
High Schools		
Business and Industry		
Adult and Community Education		
Cooperative Extension Services		
Administrative and Support Services		
Professional Support Services		

Occupational Outlook in the Profession of Education

Activity E **Name** _____ **Date** _____ **Period** _____

Part 1: Think about your future as a teacher, and then answer the following questions in the space provided.

1. What grade level(s) do you think you are interested in teaching? _____

2. Do you have an interest in certain subject areas in particular like in middle school, junior high, or high school? _____
   _____

3. What are your favorite subjects in school today? Would you be interested in teaching any of these?
   _____

4. What do you think would be the average salary for your desired teaching position? $_____

Part 2: Now, do some research using your textbook and online resources; obtain current facts about teaching.

5. What is a charter school? _____
   _____

6. What is a private school? _____
   _____

7. What is a nonsectarian school? _____
   _____

8. Some school districts contain only elementary or secondary schools, other contain both. What is a unified or unit school district?
   _____
   _____

9. How is teacher salary determined? _____
   _____

10. Teachers typically take on extra roles in their school, what are some of these positions? _____
    _____

11. While teachers get paid more to take on these additional roles, what are some other benefits to being seen in additional roles?
    _____
    _____

12. In addition to salary, what other benefits may be provided to teachers? _____
    _____

13. Considering the salary schedule shown in the text, teacher pay increases with years of experience, additional education, and in some cases for National Board Certification. Use the Internet to find out what National Board Certification is.
    _____
    _____
    _____

(Continued)

Part 3: The average teacher salary varies greatly by state as well as local community. Visit the *National Center for Education Statistics* website. Search for the "average teacher salary," open the link and take a look at the table listing the average teacher salaries in public elementary and secondary schools. Compare two or three states in which you might be interested in teaching in one day.

14. What differences do you notice right away? _____

15. Which state has the highest salary? _____

16. Which the lowest? _____

17. How much is that difference? _____

18. Would this influence your decision to take a job in those states? Why or why not? _____

    _____

Part 4: Visit the *Bureau of Labor Statistics* website. In the search box type in the teaching position in which you are most interested (elementary teacher, history teacher, etc.). Click on the link that most resembles your interest, and then answer the following questions.

19. What is the median pay listed? _____

    Is this *more* or *less* than your estimate on the front of this page? _____

20. How many jobs were held in this field? _____

21. Job Outlook refers to whether the field is growing or declining._____

    What is the job outlook for this position? _____

    What is the percentage of growth or decline? _____

22. As you click through the information, look at the similar occupations listed. Are there any that you might be interested in? List them.

    _____

    _____

    _____

23. Click on one of the similar occupations you listed. What are some aspects of the occupation that would make you consider it as a profession?

    _____

    _____

    _____

24. After reviewing the information in the text and on the websites, consider all of the benefits of teaching. What are some of the benefits that are not monetary to entering the teaching profession?

    _____

    _____

    _____

    _____

25. What might be some drawbacks or disadvantages of becoming a teacher?

    _____

    _____

    _____

    _____

Chapter 2
Becoming a Teacher

Building Your Pedagogical Vocabulary

Activity A   **Name** _____   **Date** _____   **Period** _____

As you read through Chapter 2 of the *Teaching* text, identify the vocabulary terms in the following chart. With your partner, you must:

    A. Choose and define the term

    B. Explain its value in the teaching profession

    C. Create a flash card on an 8½ - by 11-inch sheet of paper with the *term*, *definition*, and *value*

You have 15 minutes to complete this task. Once time is up, post your flash card on the board. Then take a *gallery walk*—a tour past the posted class work for reviewing and learning—to view all the flash cards and record the definitions and values in the chart that follows.

Articulate	Prerequisite course
Definition: *Value to teaching:*	*Definition:* *Value to teaching:*
Artifacts	**Philosophy of teaching**
Definition: *Value to teaching:*	*Definition:* *Value to teaching:*

(Continued)

Career goal	Personal portfolio
Definition: Value to teaching:	Definition: Value to teaching:
Grants	**Service-learning**
Definition: Value to teaching:	Definition: Value to teaching:
Job shadowing	**Proficiency tests**
Definition: Value to teaching:	Definition: Value to teaching:
Student teacher	**Teaching license**
Definition: Value to teaching:	Definition: Value to teaching:
Student teaching	**Cooperating teacher**
Definition: Value to teaching:	Definition: Value to teaching:

Steps to a Career in Education

Activity B   Name _____   Date _____   Period _____

Complete the following checklist for making the most of your high school years. As you look forward to building your educational résumé, what are you doing in high school to help prepare for your professional career? Place a check mark in the column to the left of each category item on which you are working. Write a specific notation in the right column about what actions you are taking in each category. If you are doing nothing for a category, write a goal to act on to build your strength in that area.

Check All that Apply	Categories	Actions or Goals
	Teaching Academy/Program (*this course*)	
	Teacher Education/Preparation College	
	Job Shadowing	
	Volunteering	
	Service Learning	
	Work	
	Other	

Observing Effective Teachers

Activity C   Name _____   Date _____   Period _____

In your daily experiences as a high school student, you sit in a number of classes and engage with a variety of educators. Use this as an opportunity to recognize and record the teaching styles that appeal to you. Choose the teacher from whom you feel you learn the most. During your next class with this teacher, watch for the techniques/skill sets identified in the following and, after class, record your observations. Do not identify/name the teacher or class.

1. What does the teacher do that encourages students to respond and relate to the teacher?

   _____

   _____

2. What are the teaching techniques you see (aids, materials, techniques, and technology)?

   _____

   _____

3. How is material modified for different students? (*You may not see this directly.*)

   _____

   _____

4. Does the teacher include an example or story that appeals to student interest(s)?

   _____

   _____

5. Are there class "rules" that were introduced or established in the beginning? How and what are they?

   _____

   _____

6. What are the procedures that students *just know*? For instance, how students are to turn in work or bell-work expectations.

   _____

   _____

7. How has the teacher earned the respect of the students?

   _____

   _____

8. How does the teacher demonstrate knowledge of the subject matter?

   _____

   _____

9. How does the teacher create a classroom environment conducive to learning?

   _____

   _____

10. How does the teacher exhibit sensitivity to students' diversity, gender differences, and disabilities?

   _____

   _____

Preparing for Teacher Training

Activity D   **Name** _____   **Date** _____   **Period** _____

Consider the state in which you would like to teach in some day. Look up that state's *Department of Education* on the Internet. Research teacher qualifications on the site and then answer the following questions.

1. What state are you researching and what website did you use?

   _____

   _____

2. What are the requirements to become a teacher in that state?

   _____

   _____

   _____

   _____

3. What state-required exams do you need to take in addition to having a degree?

   _____

   _____

   _____

   _____

4. Does this state offer guidance for an out-of-state certification (you get your degree in another state)? What are the requirements?

   _____

   _____

   _____

   _____

5. Many states have *endorsements* you can add to your teaching certificate. What are these?

   _____

   _____

   _____

6. If your state offers endorsements, what are the requirements to obtain one and add it to your license?

   _____

   _____

   _____

   _____

7. What benefits, if any, are there to adding endorsements or obtaining multiple certifications?

   _____

   _____

   _____

Portfolio Planning

Name _____   **Date** _____   **Period** _____

Many teacher-training programs culminate with a portfolio project during or after your student teaching experience. This course provides you with an opportunity to begin building a portfolio now. The portfolio must contain *artifacts* or examples of your work in different areas you choose to highlight. Begin documenting your experiences and abilities in the space provided, keeping in mind the areas in which you need to expand your knowledge or the experiences you need to create for yourself. Remember this is only the starting point for your portfolio.

1. List all experiences you have had working with children, (babysitting, camps, paid work, etc.) include dates and responsibilities.

   _____

   _____

   _____

2. Highlight volunteer opportunities you have participated in, (nursery care, clubs, or activities, etc.) include dates and responsibilities.

   _____

   _____

3. Identify certifications you currently hold (Red Cross Babysitter training, lifeguard, AED/CPR training, etc.).

   _____

   _____

   _____

   _____

4. List your personal leadership experiences (club or organization positions, sports teams, etc.).

   _____

   _____

   _____

5. What course(s) have you taken in high school that helped prepare you for the profession of education (*including this one*)?

   _____

   _____

   _____

   _____

6. Identify special recognitions or skills you possess (academic honors, foreign language skills).

   _____

   _____

7. Looking at the areas you highlighted above, what types of artifacts do you have that you could currently include in a portfolio? For instance, you might have certificates of achievement, photographs, or news stories.

   _____

   _____

Developing a Philosophy of Teaching

Activity F   Name _____ **Date** _____ **Period** _____

In the process of developing your *Philosophy of Teaching*, begin with answering the following questions. You may not have any ideas for some of the questions, but from observing your teachers you will gain insight into the type of teacher you want to be. This exercise will serve as the starting point for your philosophy, and you will refer to it later in the course as you write a final Philosophy of Teaching.

1. What is learning? What is teaching? _____

   _____

   _____

   _____

   _____

2. Why are learning and teaching important? _____

   _____

   _____

   _____

   _____

3. How will you challenge students? _____

   _____

   _____

   _____

   _____

4. How will you accommodate different learning styles? _____

   _____

   _____

   _____

   _____

5. How will you help students who are frustrated? _____

   _____

   _____

   _____

   _____

6. Describe how you want your students to feel in your classroom? How will you help them feel this way?

   _____

   _____

   _____

   _____

(Continued)

7. What are the goals of your classroom/students? (For example, learn content of the class or develop critical-thinking skills.)

_____

_____

_____

_____

8. How will you accomplish the goals for your classroom? _____

_____

_____

_____

_____

9. What personal characteristics do you have that influence your teaching style?

_____

_____

_____

_____

10. What type of relationship would you like to develop with your students? How will you build that relationship?

_____

_____

_____

_____

_____

11. What type of learning environment will you provide to help students learn (physical/social environment)?

_____

_____

_____

_____

12. How do you view inclusion and address diversity in your classroom? _____

_____

_____

_____

_____

Chapter 3
The Early History of Education in America

Exploring and Connecting Text

Activity A   Name _____   Date _____   Period _____

Complete the sentences that follow using *content* and *academic* terms found in text Chapter 3. Then respond to the in-depth questions proposed regarding the information.

1. Most children learned from their parents and some acquired a trade as an _____.

   What professions continue to utilize the apprenticeship model for training their workers today?

   _____

2. Few students had the opportunity to attend college, but two of the first colleges established during the *American Colonial Period* were _____ _____ and the College of _____ and _____.

   Both of these colleges continue to be held in high regard in this country. How do you think their innovative origins continue to contribute to their success?

   _____

3. Religion played a major role in the development of education, both in the drive to learn to _____ and in the development of schools that believed everyone should be educated.

   The Religious Society of Friends (of Quakers) still exists and has an established network of schools around the country. What do you think might have influenced the Quakers to start their own schools? Do you think this is still an issue today? Explain.

   _____

   _____

   _____

4. _____ was the first state to enact a law requiring schools to be available in their communities.

   This is the point in our history that government began to play a role in education. Why do you believe the government became invested in education?

   _____

   _____

5. Historically teachers were seen as important members of the community. They were expected to be _____ role models.

   How do you think the view of teachers has changed? What is the expectation of teachers as role models and what is their standing in society today?

   _____

   _____

(Continued)

6. Benjamin Franklin's role in education began when he established a school in Philadelphia. This school was different in that it did not limit attendance to those of the same beliefs and _____.

   Today especially, there is a push for more character education in schools which is part of being a good citizen. This is something that Benjamin Franklin's school first introduced to education. What is important about citizenship today and why is there a renewed focus on it in public education?

   _____

   _____

7. Horace Mann of Massachusetts worked to establish public schools that were state supported. These schools were referred to as _____ schools. They provide the same education to children from all social classes. Teacher training schools were also established during this time, they were referred to as _____ schools.

   Through the years there has been much debate about whether schools could provide the same level of education to all students when the primary source of funding was tax dollars specific to the surroundings of the school. For example a school in an area with lower household values would have less funds available than a school in an area with higher household values. Does this provide the same opportunity to all students? Explain your reaction and how you would improve the disparity.

   _____

   _____

   _____

8. Kindergarten came into American education in the 1870s via a German educator, *Friedrich Froebel.* The intention was to use songs and games—essentially play and social interactions—to help young children learn. These educational methods are still utilized today in all levels of education. Maria Montessori's program focused on sensory experiences as a method for obtaining knowledge.

   Recall a time when you learned through songs, games, social interactions, or through play. Was it a beneficial way for you to learn? Why or why not?

   _____

   _____

9. During the *American Progressive Period,* several changes took place in education. Elementary school attendance became mandatory for all children, women achieved the right to vote, public high schools emerged, and the belief that curriculum in schools needed to address societal concerns through critical thinking and problem solving became a focus.

   High schools became important in preparing students for careers right out of high school in lieu of going to college. What courses have you taken in high school that you can relate to the skills you will need after you graduate? Name the course and skill obtained and how it will help you in the world of work.

   _____

   _____

   _____

10. The economy plays a large role in education just as it does in most aspects of American life. During the Great Depression, the government stepped in to supplement schools that could not afford the cost of educating children. Today, the *National School Lunch Program* provides free or reduced-price lunches to over 30 million children.

    Present arguments to either *support* or *protest* the existence of the free/reduced lunch program.

    _____

    _____

    _____

History's Influence on Today's Education

Activity B   **Name** _____   **Date** _____   **Period** _____

Write your answers to each of the following items in the space provided.

1. From 1600 through the 1940s, the economy had an effect on education in America. Explain the impact of economic factors on education during each of the periods mentioned in the text.

   a. The American Colonial Period (1600–1776): _____

   _____

   _____

   b. The American Early National Period (1776–1840): _____ `

   _____

   _____

   c. The American Common School Period (1840–1880): _____

   _____

   _____

   d. The American Progressive Period (1880–1921): _____

   _____

   _____

   e. The 1920s and the Great Depression Era (1921–1940): _____

   _____

   _____

2. The role of teachers has been continuously evolving. Write an explanation of the evolution of the role of the teacher through history.

   _____

   _____

   _____

   _____

   _____

   _____

   _____

3. Summarize the progression of influences on the evolution school curriculums from the 1600s through the 1940s.

   _____

   _____

   _____

   _____

   _____

   _____

   _____

Researching People of Influence on Education

Activity C   **Name** _____   **Date** _____   **Period** _____

Choose one of the following people of interest to you from this chapter who played a role in education. Then conduct research, referring to the text, online sources, and personal experiences when answering the questions that follow. Be prepared to share your findings with the class.

Maria Montessori   John Dewey   Horace Mann

Friedrich Froebel   Thomas Jefferson   Benjamin Franklin

1. What was the individual's initiative (philosophy/vision/mission) that had a lasting influence on education?

   _____

   _____

   _____

   _____

2. List at least two *current* pros and two *current* cons of the initiative.

Pros	Cons

3. Why do you believe the initiative endured? Consider societal, historical, government, and other influences.

   _____

   _____

   _____

4. What statistics, studies, or *proof* exist of success or failure of the individual's initiative?

   _____

   _____

   _____

5. How do you think this initiative impacts today's educational environment?

   _____

   _____

   _____

6. Pose a question you would ask the person regarding his or her education initiative.

   _____

   _____

7. On a separate sheet of paper, create a graphic representing the influence this initiative has had on education. Attach your graphic to this activity sheet.

Chapter 4
The Modern History of Education in America

Building Your Pedagogical Vocabulary and Relating It to Your Community

Activity A   **Name** _____   **Date** _____   **Period** _____

In the space provided, write the definition of each of the following terms. Then complete the statement or activity that follows each definition.

1. *Project Head Start* is _____

   _____

   _____

   _____

   In my community an example of the Head Start program and its role in the community is (visit the Head Start website and click on "Find a Head Start Program" to locate a local program).

   _____

   _____

   _____

   _____

   _____

   _____

2. *Bilingual education* is _____

   _____

   _____

   _____

   Conduct research to locate bilingual programs available in your local schools or community. If there is a program, describe the program and who it helps. If there is not one in your area, research the closest large city and what bilingual programming it may offer.

   _____

   _____

   _____

   _____

   _____

   _____

(Continued)

3. The *back-to-basics movement* of the 1980s was aimed at erasing *illiteracy* in America. Use the Internet to locate the illiteracy rate for your state or community. Record it in the space that follows along with where you found the information.

_____

_____

As a student, what can you do to address the literacy rate in your community?

_____

_____

As a teacher, what can you do to promote literacy in your classroom?

_____

_____

4. *Educational standards* have become an important part of education. Teachers and students look to the standards for direction toward their goals. What is the significance of these standards? How do they impact your education as a student?

_____

_____

_____

_____

As a teacher, how do you think you will feel about competency-based education? Supply evidence to support your answer.

_____

_____

_____

_____

5. The *No Child Left Behind Act (NCLB)* connected standardized testing with school funding. Some people felt this was a great way to motivate educators, others felt it just put those at a disadvantage already, further behind. Provide your opinion of NCLB and provide evidence to support your position.

_____

_____

_____

_____

6. Charter schools are public schools that receive public funds, but are exempt from many of the regulations that govern traditional public schools. Charters can be revoked at any time and the schools must seek to renew their charter every so many years. This school model is fairly new and thus far there are both pros and cons as with any school model. Do charter schools exist in your community (research to find out)? If so, review their mission and comment on anything unique you come across. If none exist in your community, find one in another state and review its mission and vision.

_____

_____

_____

_____

Exploring and Connecting the Text to Your Community

Activity B   **Name** _____   **Date** _____   **Period** _____

Think about the national problem of *illiteracy*. This is considered an *at-risk* attribute, meaning those students who come from families who cannot read or write English enter school with a disadvantage. With what you learned about illiteracy from the text and *Activity A* in this chapter, write your answers to the following questions and statements regarding literacy in your state or community. Use the Internet for research and make sure you note the sites from which you gathered information at the end of the activity. Before you get started, use the search engine of your choice to locate the four-minute video (by *Statisticks Storytelling*), *Statisticks of Lake County, IL*, to understand the snowball effect illiteracy has on children.

1. How big is the problem in your state? [Search: *illiteracy in (insert your state here)*]. Record the statistics and other information in the space that follows.

   _____
   _____
   _____
   _____

2. Detail two goals you could set to address the problem in your state.

   a. _____
   _____
   _____
   _____

   b. _____
   _____
   _____
   _____

3. List at least three possible actions that can begin to help remedy the problem of illiteracy.

   a. _____
   _____
   _____
   _____

   b. _____
   _____
   _____
   _____

   c. _____
   _____
   _____
   _____

(Continued)

4. Evaluate your actions from item #3 by listing the pros and cons for each action in the space provided.

Action (from Item 3)	Pros	Cons

5. Based on your pros/cons list, develop a plan for implementation of the action that seems most likely to be successful.

_____

_____

_____

_____

_____

_____

_____

_____

_____

6. If your action was put into place, describe how you would evaluate the end results.

_____

_____

_____

_____

_____

_____

7. List the websites and sources used to obtain information:

_____

_____

Exploring State and National Standards in Education

Activity C   **Name** _____   **Date** _____   **Period** _____

Beginning in 1991, Congress started acting on the call for educational standards to help teachers better define what students should know and be able to do on completion of each course/grade. National standards exist but so do state standards. Use the Internet to further explore the standards your state uses.

1. Which courses of study have standards in your state (English, Mathematics, Physical Education, etc.)?

   Education standards in (insert your state): _____

   _____

   _____

   _____

   _____

2. In most cases, educational standards do not dictate *how* to reach the end goal—they just express what the end goal is. Write three pros to this factor and three cons.

   Pros: _____

   _____

   _____

   _____

   Cons: _____

   _____

   _____

   _____

3. Competency-based education—also referred to as *teaching to the test*—is very controversial. In addition, in some states the student scores on standards-based tests are tied to teacher salary. Look online for more information. Give one positive statement and one negative statement regarding this correlation.

   Positive: _____

   _____

   _____

   Negative: _____

   _____

   _____

4. Cite evidence to support your personal feelings about teacher evaluations being partially based on student test scores.

   _____

   _____

   _____

   _____

Considering Options with Career Clusters

Activity D   Name _____ **Date** _____ **Period** _____

Becoming an educator is a terrific profession, and skills you learn in this course are highly transferable to other careers. What if, however, you still are unsure about a career in education? Career clusters are a way to help you consider other options. Complete the following items and record your responses in the space provided.

1. Visit *Career Clusters/NASDCTEc* website for your state. Read through the state profile and list three new pieces of information you learned about CTE (career and technical education) in your state.

   _____

   _____

   _____

2. After reading through the page on your state, what is one question you have about the information provided?

   _____

   _____

3. On the Career Clusters/NASDCTEc website home page, type *student survey* in the search box. Click on the *Student Interest Survey*, and when the survey opens, read through it and record your responses in the space provided.

Box	Total Number of Items of Interest per Box	Box	Total Number of Items of Interest per Box
1		9	
2		10	
3		11	
4		12	
5		13	
6		14	
7		15	
8		16	

4. In what three boxes did you have the highest number? List the names of those career clusters in the following space.

   _____

   _____

   _____

5. Identify your highest-interest cluster. On the website home page, click on the cluster link and review the information. Then click on the "Common Career Technical Core performance elements" link and review the skill requirements. In the space that follows, list each skill and note why you think each skill is important to your particular career/career cluster of choice.

   _____

   _____

   _____

   _____

   _____

Chapter 5
Schools and Society

State-level Government and Its Role in Education

Activity A   **Name** _____   **Date** _____   **Period** _____

Government plays a large role in education, both in funding and policy. Find your *State Board of Education* website (or the board of education in a state in which you would like to teach). Write your answer to the following prompts in the space provided.

1. List the website(s) you used to find information and what state you are researching.

   _____

   _____

2. Name one of the most recent laws regarding education passed by your state government.

   a. Include the official name as well as a synopsis of the law.

   _____

   _____

   _____

   b. How will the law apply to your eventual role in education?

   _____

   _____

   _____

   c. Is there a monetary amount tied to this legislation? If so explain.

   _____

   _____

   _____

3. The board of education may be elected or appointed.

   a. How are the board members determined in your state?

   _____

   b. Do the members represent certain regions of your state? If so, explain how they are divided.

   _____

   _____

   c. What is a current topic for which the board of education is advocating?

   _____

   _____

The State Department of Education

The state department of education provides essential functions that you as a future teacher should become familiar with. Find your state's department of education website and respond to the following.

1. List five important functions of your state department of education.

   _____

   _____

   _____

   _____

   _____

2. Explain in detail the steps to become a certified teacher in your state.

   _____

   _____

   _____

   _____

   _____

   _____

3. What testing, if any, must you pass in order to become a teacher in addition to your college degree? Are test preparation materials available to you? Is there a cost associated with the testing?

   _____

   _____

   _____

   _____

4. Once you meet the criteria for a teaching license, what must you do to maintain your license?

   _____

   _____

   _____

5. In addition to teaching licensure, your state department of education also regulates substitute teachers, paraprofessionals, and administrators. Describe how the department guides these professionals.

   _____

   _____

   _____

   _____

Your Local School Board

Current issues facing your school board impact your education as a student and the work environment and expectations of school staff. Learning more about how your school board functions is part of good citizenship. Write your responses to the following questions and statements in the space provided.

1. Who are your school board members? _____

   _____

   _____

   _____

   _____

   _____

2. What are the qualifications to be a school board member? _____

   _____

   _____

   _____

   _____

   _____

3. When and where are school board meetings held? _____

   _____

4. What topics were addressed on the latest school board agenda? _____

   _____

   _____

   _____

   _____

   _____

   _____

5. Choose one of the topics that interest you and delve into it further. What can you learn? Who is impacted by the decision made? Do finances play a role in the discussion?

   _____

   _____

   _____

   _____

   _____

Interview a School Board Member

Activity D   **Name** _____ **Date** _____ **Period** _____

Identify a member of your local school board you would like to interview. Contact the school board member to set up a time and place for the interview. Write your answers to the interview questions in the space that follows.

1. What are the requirements to become a board member? _____

_____

_____

_____

2. What motivated you to become a board member? _____

_____

_____

_____

3. What are the board's responsibilities? _____

_____

_____

_____

4. What is your vision for education? _____

_____

_____

_____

5. What is the role of the board in day-to-day operation of the school? _____

_____

_____

_____

6. What are the some current challenges facing our school? _____

_____

_____

_____

7. (Develop an additional question based on your research in Activity C.) _____

   Q. _____

   A. _____

_____

_____

_____

_____

Documenting Organizational Structure

Research the organizational structure of your school district. Complete the chart that follows, adding levels and labeling as needed until you account for all staff employed by the district. Some other positions you *might* add to the chart include: Principal(s), Directors, Administrators, Teachers, Support Staff, Contracted Student-Services Providers, and more. List three main responsibilities next to each position on your chart. Then write a reflective paragraph summarizing your understanding of the school district organization and how this organization benefits students, teachers, and parents.

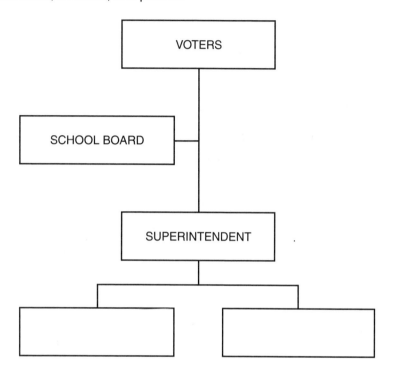

School Funding in Your District or State

Name _____   **Date** _____   **Period** _____

Funding of public education varies throughout the country. Complete the following to determine how your school district or state funds schools.

Part 1: Research how education is funded in either your school district or your state and write the percentages in the space that follows (check one: _____my school district; _____my state).

1. *Federal* funding percentage: _____

2. *State* funding percentage: _____

3. *Local* funding percentage: _____

4. *Private* funding percentage:_____

5. *Other* funding percentage:_____

Part 2: Create a pie chart with a color key that shows the above percentages for your district or state.

☐	Federal funding
☐	State funding
☐	Local funding
☐	Private funding
☐	Other

Part 3: Then write your response to the questions or statements that follow.

6. Cite your sources: _____

_____

_____

7. What is the spending per pupil in your school district or state? _____

_____

8. Explain the most interesting part of school funding you discovered. _____

_____

_____

_____

Data Analysis and Inequality in Funding

Activity G **Name** _____ **Date** _____ **Period** _____

There many contributing factors to student success. How important is funding in that equation? Complete the chart that follows by searching online for the **largest** school district in your state, the **smallest** school district, a **rural** school district, and a **suburban** school district. Then complete the questions that follow the chart. You can use a specific district if you know one or do a general Internet search using the chart headings. Many states have one site that displays the information; for other states you may have to look on each district's website. Median home values can be found on several websites—ask your teacher for guidance. A sample has been provided; include source citations at teacher request.

	Spending per Pupil	Graduation Rate	Average ACT or SAT Score	Students Eligible for Free or Reduced Lunch	Median Home Value
SAMPLE **Washington, DC**	$8,739 District of Columbia Public Schools, website, Data-at-a-glance	58% District of Columbia Public Schools, website, Data-at-a-glance	16.2 District of Columbia, Office of the State Superintendent of Education website	76% District of Columbia Public Schools, website	$480,000 Zillow website, Washington, DC home values
Largest District _____ (Name of District)					
Smallest District _____ (Name of District)					
Rural District _____ (Name of District)					
Suburban District _____ (Name of District)					

(Continued)

Answer the following questions based on your research.

1. Based on your research, how is *Spending per Pupil* related to *Graduation Rate*?

_____

_____

_____

_____

2. What conclusions can you draw regarding *Students Eligible* and *Average ACT or SAT Score*?

_____

_____

_____

_____

3. Can you propose an alternative way to fund or supplement current funding for education?

_____

_____

_____

_____

_____

_____

_____

4. What is the relationship between *Median Home Value* and *Graduation Rate*? Why is this important?

_____

_____

_____

_____

5. Correlate the school *funding gap* and the *achievement gap*.

_____

_____

_____

_____

_____

_____

_____

Societal Problems Affecting Schools

Activity H   Name _____   Date _____   Period _____

Part 1: For each of the terms that follow, write what the term means in an educational setting. Then find out what your school's policies are regarding how staff addresses the problem. Briefly describe the school policies and list any programs in place to assist students affected. Write your findings in the space provided.

Societal Problem	How Staff Address the Problem
Poverty	
At-risk	
Intimidation	
Bullying	
Cyberbullying	
Sexual harassment	
Racial harassment	
Physical violence	

(Continued)

Part 2: Complete the following. Write your answers in the space provided.

1. Choose one of the societal problems described that you have had a personal experience with. Without giving identifying information, briefly describe the incident.

   _____

   _____

   _____

   _____

   _____

2. Explain how the adults involved responded to the incident.

   _____

   _____

   _____

   _____

   _____

3. As a teacher, how would you address the problem taking into account all parties and school policy?

   _____

   _____

   _____

   _____

   _____

4. Design a school program that could address the problem through conflict resolution or some other design to aide students who might face a similar struggle.

   _____

   _____

   _____

   _____

   _____

   _____

   _____

   _____

   _____

   _____

   _____

   _____

   _____

Chapter 6
Understanding Human Development

Building Your Pedagogical Vocabulary

Name _____ **Date** _____ **Period** _____

Part 1: Choose one important term from this chapter. Do the following:

    A. Define the term

    B. Provide an example of the word in context

    C. Supply a visual representation of the term

You will have 15 minutes to complete this task and then present your term to the class.

Part 2: While others are presenting, write their definitions, context that makes sense to you, and describe their visuals in the space provided.

Term	Definition	Context	Visual
Growth			
Development			
Physical development			
Gross-motor skills			
Fine-motor skills			
Cognition			

(Continued)

Term	Definition	Context	Visual
Cognitive development			
Social-emotional development			
Behaviorism			
Classical conditioning			
Operant conditioning			
Constructivism			
Experiential learning			
Socratic learning			
Psychosocial theory			
Moral development			
Sociocultural theory			

Pavlov's Classical Conditioning and Skinner's Operant Conditioning

Activity B   Name _____   Date _____   Period _____

Part 1: With a partner or team, choose either Pavlov or Skinner to investigate using print and Internet resources. Brainstorm a way to demonstrate your researcher's conditioning principle. Plan your video using the guidelines and prompts that follow. Make sure your research is complete and that the video will effectively portray an example of your theorists' principle in action! (For example, how could you use either theory to get children to clean up at the end of an activity? Is flashing lights, counting down, etc., an example of conditioning?)

Partner or team members: _____

Theorist: _____

Principle: _____

   1. Brainstorm three ways you could demonstrate this type of conditioning *in a classroom*.

      a. _____

      b. _____

      c. _____

   2. Choose one of your three ideas above to demonstrate in the video. Place a check mark beside your choice.

   3. Outline a script for your video.

      a. What needs to be demonstrated? _____

      _____

      _____

      _____

      b. How will you demonstrate these concepts? _____

      _____

      _____

      _____

      c. What dialog (if any) will you include? _____

      _____

      _____

      _____

   4. Who will record the video, and who will be in the video (if needed)? _____

      _____

   5. What props or items will you need to complete your video? Who will be responsible to bring these items?

      _____

   6. Create your own definition of this type of conditioning to include in your video.

      _____

Part 2: Create your video using school-approved video and web applications for your video. Show your video to the class. Does the class agree your video shows an effective example of your theorist's principle? Why or why not?

Theorist Biographies

With a partner, choose a theorist from this chapter (Bandura, Pavlov, Piaget, Bruner, Vygotsky, Kolb, Erikson, or Kohlberg). Then do the following:

Part 1: Complete the following plan outlining your theorist's biography. Use the text and Internet resources to complete your plan.

1. Theorist: _____

2. Occupation: _____

3. Birth date/date of death: _____

4. Country of origin: _____

5. Educational background: _____

   _____

   _____

6. When and where the theorist developed the theory: _____

   _____

   _____

7. Name and explanation of theory: _____

   _____

   _____

   _____

8. Additional notable career events: _____

   _____

9. Your personal opinion of the theory (agree/disagree), and why. _____

   _____

   _____

   _____

10. What pictures or graphics regarding your theorist would enhance your visual? _____

   _____

11. How can this theory be helpful in the classroom as a teacher? _____

   _____

   _____

   _____

Part 2: Create a visual display (a poster or a digital poster) or presentation of the information after gathering data and completing the plan. Make sure your display or presentation contains all the data you have gathered and that you **understand** the material. You must be able to differentiate your theorist's biography and theory from others your classmates are presenting. If creating a digital poster, use a school-approved application.

Part 3: Present your theorist's biography to the class.

Erikson's Psychosocial Theory

Activity D   **Name** _____   **Date** _____   **Period** _____

Throughout your life you have gone through many physical, emotional, and social developmental milestones, and there are others you anticipate as you age. Consider the time line on the next page, which begins with birth and ends with death. There have been many studies regarding the relationships between these milestones and emotional and social development. Use the following directions to learn more about *Erikson's Psychosocial Theory*, an example has been started for you.

1. Brainstorm some milestones humans go through (examples: first steps, first words, first day of school, puberty, first date, graduations, college, first job, marriage, children, careers, home ownership, retirement, and others).

_____

_____

_____

_____

_____

_____

_____

_____

_____

_____

_____

_____

_____

_____

2. List a milestone event that occurs during each stage of *Psychosocial Development* in the space provided in the time line.

3. Identify each milestone as *physical, emotional, social,* or a *combination*.

4. Write the name of Erickson's developmental stage and task associated with each milestone.

    a. Infancy *(Trust vs. Mistrust)*

    b. Toddler *(Autonomy vs. Shame and Doubt)*

    c. Early Childhood *(Initiative vs. Guilt)*

    d. Middle Childhood *(Industry vs. Inferiority)*

    e. Adolescence *(Identity vs. Role Confusion)*

    f. Young Adulthood *(Intimacy vs. Isolation)*

    g. Middle Adulthood *(Generativity vs. Self-Absorption)*

    h. Older Adulthood *(Integrity vs. Despair)*

5. Write a brief description of the stage in your own words.

6. Provide a pictorial representation of the stage.

(Continued)

Milestone	Physical, Social, Emotional, or Combination	Erikson's Developmental Stage	Description of Developmental Stage	Visual to Represent Stage
Birth	Physical	Infancy Trust vs. Mistrust	When caregivers meet their needs, babies learn trust. Babies perceive the world as an unpredictable place when their needs are not met.	
_____				
_____				
_____				
_____				
_____				
_____				
Death				

Chapter 7
Middle Childhood: Growth and Development

Visual Vocabulary

Activity A   Name _____   Date _____   Period _____

Part 1: Write the definition of each term in your own words in the chart below. Look for pictures or video clips that demonstrate the term and cite your sources in the space provided.

Term	My Definition	Picture/Clip to Represent and URL of Image or Video Clip
Classification		
Conservation		
Developmental delay		
Dexterity		
Executive strategies		
Hand-eye coordination		

(Continued)

Term	My Definition	Picture/Clip to Represent and URL of Image or Video Clip
Proficient		
Self-concept		
Seriation		
Transitivity		
Visual-motor coordination		

Part 2: Choose one of the following options and create a visual that demonstrates each of the academic terms in the previous chart. Share your visual-vocabulary project with the class.

    A. Develop a video montage by using the software of your choice to string together video clips of each term being demonstrated.

    B. Create a collage with pictures from magazines or printed from the Internet that demonstrate each term.

Observation with Purpose (Ages 5–7)

Activity B   Name _____ Date _____ Period _____

Each day you observe a variety of behaviors, some you understand, and some you do not. After reading the text, you will gain a deeper understanding of the behaviors of children at different ages. Chapter 7 *Activities B, C,* and *D* are designed to focus your observations. Read the questions thoroughly before beginning and plan a minimum of 30 minutes to complete each observation. Here are some ways you can complete your observations.

- **A: Cooperating classroom.** Explain your assignment to your cooperating teacher and observe the students. Complete the activity for their age group (Activity B, C, or D). Then switch places (with teacher permission) with another student who is placed in a different age-level classroom and observe there, too.
- **B: Volunteering.** You can volunteer at an afterschool program, at a religious organization, babysit, or in some other capacity where you can observe children. Share your assignment with parents and program coordinators to gain permission to observe the children in the age range of each activity.
- **C: Networking.** Use your networking skills and ask friends and family members with children in the age range you need to observe. Make sure, once again, you share the focus of the observation and gain permission.

Observation Tips

- Plan for a 30 minute observation period.
- Do not share what you observe outside of your classroom environment. *Confidentiality* is a MUST!
- NEVER use the child's name.
- Complete your observations from a distance so the child/children do not know you are watching.
- Avoid comparing children or making assumptions about their behavior.
- Be objective! Observations are statements of fact, not opinion.

Complete the following observation. Write your responses in the space provided.

Observation environment: _____

Date of observation: _____   Time of observation: _____

Approximate age of child: _____   Gender of child: _____

1. List the gross-motor skills you see the child display. Check (✓) the ones the child is still developing and star (*) the ones the child has mastered.

   ☐ A. _____   ☐ D. _____

   ☐ B _____   ☐ E _____

   ☐ C. _____   ☐ F. _____

2. Choose one of the gross-motor skills and describe the action in factual detail.

   _____
   _____
   _____
   _____
   _____

(Continued)

3. Describe the hand-eye coordination you witness the child demonstrating and what activity they are accomplishing.

_____

_____

_____

4. Describe the child's self-help skills you observed him/her completing.

_____

_____

_____

5. Consider the child's cognitive development; cite an example of a time it appeared the child was thinking about a situation, idea, etc.

_____

_____

_____

_____

6. If you observe the child reading, report on what you observed, their level of confidence in their reading and how they managed words they were unfamiliar with.

_____

_____

_____

7. Explain an interaction, you observed, between the child and one of his/her peers.

_____

_____

_____

_____

8. If the child demonstrated in some way insight into their self-concept, detail their actions and your _hypothesis_ about the meaning.

_____

_____

_____

9. Is this child able to wait their turn when playing or working with their peers? Are they able to share if needed? In what ways did the child demonstrate an ability to cooperate with others?

_____

_____

_____

10. Does the child exhibit any disabilities or other factors that may impede his/her progression at an average rate?

_____

_____

_____

Observation with Purpose (Ages 8–9)

Activity C   **Name** _____ **Date** _____ **Period** _____

Refer to the observation guidelines presented in *Activity B,* and then complete the following observation. Write your responses in the space provided.

Observation environment: _____

Date of observation: _____ Time of observation: _____

Approximate age of child: _____ Gender of child: _____

1. List the gross-motor skills you see the child display. Check (✓) the ones the child is still developing and star (*) the ones the child has mastered.

   ☐ A. _____   ☐ D _____

   ☐ B _____   ☐ E _____

   ☐ C. _____   ☐ F. _____

2. Choose one of the gross-motor skills and describe the action in factual detail.

   _____

   _____

   _____

   _____

3. Describe the hand-eye coordination you witness the child demonstrating and what activity they are accomplishing.

   _____

   _____

   _____

   _____

4. Consider the child's cognitive development; cite an example of a time it appeared the child was thinking about a situation, idea, etc.

   _____

   _____

   _____

   _____

5. If you are fortunate to observe the child learning with the use of actual objects, describe the demonstration of seriation, classification, conservation, or transitivity.

   _____

   _____

   _____

   _____

(Continued)

6. If you observe the child reading, report on what you observed. Was the child able to identify main points, summarize, and make predictions about the text?

_____

_____

_____

_____

_____

_____

7. Explain an interaction you observed between the child and one of his/her peers.

_____

_____

_____

_____

_____

_____

8. If the child demonstrated in some way insight into their self-concept, detail their actions and your _hypothesis_ about the meaning.

_____

_____

_____

_____

_____

_____

9. Revisit Kohlberg's preconventional level of moral development. Does the child follow the rules selectively? Does the child try to negotiate for a benefit?

_____

_____

_____

_____

_____

_____

10. Does the child exhibit any disabilities or other factors that may impede his/her progression at an average rate?

_____

_____

_____

_____

_____

_____

Observation with Purpose (Ages 10–12)

Activity D   **Name** _____   **Date** _____   **Period** _____

Refer to the observation guidelines presented in *Activity B,* and then complete the following observation. Write your responses in the space provided.

Observation environment: _____

Date of observation: _____   Time of observation: _____

Approximate age of child: _____   Gender of child: _____

1. List the gross-motor skills you see the child display. Check (✓) the ones the child is still developing and star (*) the ones the child has mastered.

   ☐ A. _____   ☐ D _____

   ☐ B _____   ☐ E _____

   ☐ C. _____   ☐ F. _____

2. Choose one of the gross-motor skills and describe the action in factual detail.

   _____

   _____

   _____

   _____

3. Consider the child's cognitive development; cite an example of a time it appeared the child was thinking about a situation, idea, etc.

   _____

   _____

   _____

   _____

4. Detail the process of decision making you observe the child engage in. This could be a small quick decision or a more specific problem they are addressing. Make sure you record oral evidence as well as physical response or nonverbal cues the child may display.

   _____

   _____

   _____

   _____

5. If you observe the child reading, report on what you observed. Did the child appear to enjoy reading? What signs indicate their feelings about reading?

   _____

   _____

   _____

   _____

(Continued)

6. Explain an interaction you observed between the child and one of his/her peers.

_____

_____

_____

_____

_____

7. Explain an interaction you observed between the child and a *group* of his or her peers.

_____

_____

_____

_____

_____

8. If the child demonstrated in some way insight into their self-concept, detail their actions and your *hypothesis* about the meaning.

_____

_____

_____

_____

_____

9. Consider both Kohlberg's preconventional and conventional stages of moral development. Does the child follow the rules selectively? Does the child try to negotiate for a benefit? Does the child base decisions on the perception of a "good" or "bad" response?

_____

_____

_____

_____

_____

10. Does the child exhibit any disabilities or other factors that may impede his/her progression at an average rate?

_____

_____

_____

_____

_____

Connecting to Your Own Life

Activity E   **Name** _____ **Date** _____ **Period** _____

Part 1: Now that you have learned so much about development through middle childhood, apply this knowledge to your own life. Create a visual of your life using a digital program of your choice. Then the class will do a gallery walk to view each other's presentations. Use the following information to create the plan for your visual. Write your answers in the space provided.

1. Your name: _____

2. Describe where you were born: _____

3. Include information about your family: _____

4. Explain the environment you grew up in as a child, including how it may have changed:

    _____

    _____

5. Identify important events and memories from your childhood to the present, from each of the stages from age 5–12, including:

    a. Physical growth and development: _____

        _____

    b. Gross-motor skills: _____

        _____

    c. Fine-motor skills: _____

        _____

    d. Cognitive development: _____

        _____

    e. Social-emotional development: _____

        _____

    f. Peer relationships: _____

        _____

    g. Family relationships: _____

        _____

    h. Self-concept: _____

        _____

    i. Moral development: _____

        _____

6. Include childhood photos (if possible), video clips, or photos of artifacts that represent different stages of your childhood.

Part 2: Refer to the rubric on the following page for specific information regarding your performance expectations and grading. Once you have completed your visual presentation, use the rubric to self-grade and reflect on your work and determine if it meets expectations. Place a check (✓) over the performance level (*Advanced, Proficient, Developing, Incomplete*) you think you achieved for each criteria.

(Continued)

Rubric—Connecting to Your Own Life

Criteria	Advanced	Proficient	Developing	Incomplete
Information	Contains name, descriptive information regarding place of birth, family, and living environment, and how they may have changed over time.	Contains name, descriptive information regarding place of birth, family, and living environment, and how they may have changed over time. Minor deficiencies in information.	One to two pieces of information are minimal or missing, such as name, descriptive information regarding place of birth, family, or living environment, and how they may have changed over time.	Several pieces of required information are missing or inadequate. Descriptions are lacking or minimal.
Physical Growth and Development	Examples and explanations of physical growth and development are provided at three different stages; includes fine- and gross-motor skills.	Examples and explanations of physical growth and development are provided at two to three different stages; includes fine- and gross-motor skills.	Examples and explanations of physical growth and development are lacking, but are provided at one to two different stages. Fine- or gross-motor skills may be missing from presentation.	Examples and explanations of physical growth and development are inadequate. Not all stages are addressed. Fine- and/or gross-motor skills are missing from presentation.
Cognitive Development	Examples and explanations of cognitive growth and development are provided at three different stages.	Examples and explanations of cognitive growth and development are provided at two different stages.	Examples and explanations of cognitive growth and development are lacking, but are provided at one to two different stages.	Examples and explanations of cognitive growth and development are inadequate. Not all stages are addressed.
Social-Emotional Development	Examples and explanations of social-emotional growth and development are provided at all three stages, including peer and family relationships and self-concept.	Examples and explanations of social-emotional growth and development are provided at two different stages, including peer and family relationships and self-concept.	Examples and explanations of social-emotional growth and development are lacking, but are provided at two different stages. Peer and family relationships or self-concept may be missing from presentation.	Examples and explanations of social-emotional growth and development are inadequate. One to two stages are addressed. Peer and family relationships or self-concept may be missing from presentation.
Moral Development	Examples and explanations of moral development are provided at three different stages.	Examples and explanations of moral development are provided at two different stages.	Examples and explanations of moral development are provided at one stage *or* examples and explanations are lacking.	Examples and explanations of moral development are inadequate.
Visuals	Visuals are used to enhance understanding on all but one or two topics. Audio, pictures, and backgrounds are appropriate and enhance the information.	Visuals are used to enhance understanding on all but three topics. Audio, pictures, and backgrounds are appropriate and enhance the information.	Visuals are used to enhance understanding only a few topics. Audio, pictures, and backgrounds are appropriate and enhance the information.	Visuals are lacking on most topics. Audio, pictures, or backgrounds are inappropriate and detract from the information.
Format and Mechanics (Spelling, grammar, and punctuation)	Commentary and text contain no major errors and minor errors do not interfere with information.	Commentary and text contain one to two major errors and other errors do not significantly interfere with information.	Commentary and text contains three to four major errors and other errors which interfere with communication of the material.	Numerous errors in text and commentary which create difficulty in interpreting the material.

Chapter 8
The Teen Years: Growth and Development

Building Your Pedagogical Vocabulary

Activity A   Name _____   Date _____   Period _____

As you read through Chapter 8 of the *Teaching* text, identify the vocabulary terms in the following chart. Individually or with your partner, you must:

A. Choose and define the term

B. Explain its value in the teaching profession

C. Create a flash card on an 8½- by 11-inch sheet of paper with the *term*, *definition*, and *value*

You have 15 minutes to complete this task. Once time is up, post your flash card on the board. Then take a *gallery walk*—a tour past the posted class work for reviewing and learning—to view all the flash cards and record the definitions and values in the chart that follows.

Puberty *Definition:* *Value to teaching:*	**Growth spurts** *Definition:* *Value to teaching:*
Asynchrony *Definition:* *Value to teaching:*	**Egocentrism** *Definition:* *Value to teaching:*

(Continued)

Metacognition *Definition:* *Value to teaching:*	**Gray matter** *Definition:* *Value to teaching:*
Amygdala *Definition:* *Value to teaching:*	**Prefrontal cortex** *Definition:* *Value to teaching:*
Neural connections *Definition:* *Value to teaching:*	**Autonomy** *Definition:* *Value to teaching:*
Multitasking *Definition:* *Value to teaching:*	**Resilience** *Definition:* *Value to teaching:*
Hypocrisy *Definition:* *Value to teaching:*	**Invincibility** *Definition:* *Value to teaching:*

Understanding the Adolescent Brain

Activity B   **Name** _____   **Date** _____   **Period** _____

Part 1: Based on your reading of the text regarding the brain, you should be able to identify several ways adolescents use and develop their brains. Review the following image. Use page 186 of the text and Internet resources to identify characteristics adolescents display to demonstrate the development in each part of the brain identified below.

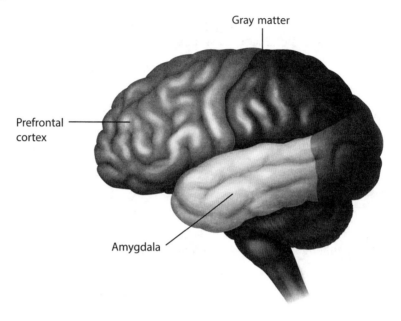

1. Prefrontal cortex—how development is demonstrated: _____

   _____

   _____

   _____

2. Gray matter—how development is demonstrated: _____

   _____

   _____

   _____

3. Amygdala—how development is demonstrated: _____

   _____

   _____

   _____

4. Neural connections—how development is demonstrated: _____

   _____

   _____

   _____

Part 2: *Optional:* Interview an adolescent about the decisions he or she makes, what guides his or her decisions, and how he or she controls or exhibits emotions. Record his or her responses in on a separate sheet of paper and attach it to this activity sheet.

Metacognition in Teaching

Activity C   Name _____ Date _____ Period _____

Part 1: Metacognition refers to the way people think about their own cognitive processes. Why people think, learn, process information, problem solve the way they do, as well as their ability to transfer knowledge to a new context is all part of metacognition. In this activity, you will be analyzing your own metacognitive strategy. You will set a goal, self-assess, adapt, and then reassess your goal.

1. Consider an area in school with which you struggle. Perhaps it is a certain subject, a specific type of task, the current unit in a certain class, etc. Choose one area to focus on today and write your goal here:

   _____

   _____

2. *Pre-assess:* your current view of the task/topic you wrote above. What do you already know about the topic that will help direct your learning?

   _____

   _____

   _____

   _____

Part 2: Now perform the task, attend the class, or take another action. Then write your responses to the following questions.

3. What was most confusing part of the material presented or task today? _____

   _____

   _____

   _____

4. *Adapt:* How can you link your prior knowledge (question 2) to the material/task of today (question 3)?

   _____

   _____

   _____

Part 3: *Post-assessment:* Write your answers to the following questions and statements in the space provided.

5. Before this course, I thought __**a.**__ was __**b.**__ . Now I think that __**c.**__ is __**d.**__ .

   a. _____

   b. _____

   c. _____

   d. _____

6. My thinking has changed in this way: _____

   _____

   _____

7. As a future teacher, how can this process help your students? _____

   _____

   _____

Social-Emotional and Moral Development in the Teen Years

Activity D   Name _____ Date _____ Period _____

Part 1: For each of the topics about teens in the following chart, identify the characteristics of growth and development, common struggles teens have in each area, and strategies teachers can use to assist students. Write your responses in the space provided.

Topic	Growth or Development in Teens	Common Struggle in This Area	Strategies for Teachers to Assist Students
Redefining self			
Moving toward independence			
Peer relationships			
Romantic relationships			

(Continued)

Topic	Growth or Development in Teens	Common Struggle in This Area	Strategies for Teachers to Assist Students
Family relationships			
Emotional challenges			
Personal values			

Part 2: Choose one of the topics from the preceding chart. Create a poster (digitally or using poster board) that meets the criteria in the following list. Then, in the space provided, plan and draw a sketch showing how your illustrations and written copy will be arranged on the poster. Present your poster and information to the class.

1. Explains the development and growth during the teen years for the topic.

2. Illustrates common struggles teens face regarding the topic.

3. Provides strategies for teachers to assist students who face a struggle in the area defined.

4. Contains all content necessary to understand and apply the topic and is professional and neat in composition.

Chapter 9
Teaching Diverse Learners

Building Your Pedagogical Vocabulary

Activity A   Name _____   Date _____   Period _____

Part 1: As you read through Chapter 9 of the *Teaching* text, you will come across several terms that will play an important role in your day-to-day activities as an educator. Pay special attention to these terms. With a partner, you must: define the term(s) and locate a short, school-appropriate video clip online that demonstrates the usage of these terms in an educational setting. Write the definitions of the terms and the video URLs in the space provided in the chart that follows.

TERM	Definition	Visual (URL)
Learning diversity		
Learning styles		
Visual learners		
Kinesthetic-tactile learners		
Differentiated instruction		
Multiple intelligences		
Exceptional learners		
Special needs		

(Continued)

TERM	Definition	Visual (URL)
Individualized Education Program (IEP)		
Accommodations		
Mainstreaming		
Inclusion		
Special education		
Limited English Proficiency (LEP)		
English Language Learners (ELL)		
Motivation		
Ethnicity		
Arduous		
Stereotype		

Part 2: Choose one term and one video from the preceding chart that you and your partner will present to the class. List the term and the URL of the video clip in the space provided as follows. Discuss with the class how the video supports the definition of the term.

Term: _____

URL of video clip: _____

_____

_____

Observing Learning Styles

Name _____   **Date** _____   **Period** _____

Part 1: In the classroom in which you are an intern or cadet, spend one day *just* observing 10 students during a traditional lesson and focus on their learning styles. Write the students initials (or assign each student a letter) in the following chart prior to your observation. Place a tally mark in the table each time you see the child grasping a concept or choosing one of the methods of learning—*Visual, Kinesthetic,* or *Verbal.* For at least three of the students, record a brief summary of what you saw that indicated a preference for a particular learning style. Answer the questions that follow after you have completed the observation.

Student Identification	Tally					Summary of Observation
	Visual	**Kinesthetic**	**Verbal**	

(Continued)

Student Identification	Tally ЖЖ			Summary of Observation
	Visual	Kinesthetic	Verbal	

1. Analyze the data you have collected. Which learning style appears to be the **most** prevalent in the class? Does this surprise you; why or why not? Comment on your observations.

_____

_____

_____

_____

_____

2. Which learning style did you record the **least** number of students using? What impact could this knowledge have on the students? How could it relate to the way you present a lesson?

_____

_____

_____

_____

_____

Part 2: To take this lesson to the next level, ask permission of your cooperating teacher ahead of time to revise the lesson you will be observing to give students a choice of lesson activities (visual, kinesthetic, or verbal) to allow you to correlate student activity choices to their learning styles.

3. If you modified the lesson to allow the students a choice of learning activities, explain what you did and the potential impact on student learning. If you did not modify the lesson, explain what you would have done to provide students with an option of learning activities to meet their personal learning styles.

_____

_____

_____

_____

_____

_____

Applying Multiple Intelligences to the Classroom

Activity C   Name _____   Date _____   Period _____

Part 1: Individually, with a partner, or in a small group, design a lesson based on the story of *Cinderella*, or another fairy tale your teacher assigns. Choose one of the multiple intelligences (or use the one your teacher assigns). Outline the lesson details that include a specific activity relating to your chosen *intelligence*. (*Note*: A sample is provided, in greater detail than required of you.)

SAMPLE Lesson
Lesson Title: Intrapersonal—Cinderella Wants to Go to the Ball
Goals/Outcomes: The students will be able to brainstorm possible solutions, demonstrate the concept of goal driven decisions, reflect on possible solutions and analyze options.
The Opportunity for a Solution: Cinderella wants to attend the ball but she does not have money or time to prepare herself. Without a fairy godmother, what other ways can Cinderella attend the ball?
Learning Activities: • 3 minutes—Introduce the opportunity for a solution.   • 5 minutes—Brainstorm and record solutions as a class, do not evaluate them.   • 5–7 minutes—Each student writes in his or her own personal journal starting with this prompt: *Cinderella's goal is to attend the ball, if I were her I would…*   • 2 minutes—Ask students to share which solution they chose.   • 7–10 minutes—Direct students to write in their journals using this prompt: *Considering other solutions, reflect on the solution you chose and compare and contrast the projected course of action with another option you are aware of.*   • 5 minutes—Optional sharing of outcomes and options as closure.

Complete a plan using your chosen or assigned intelligence. Brainstorm ideas yourself or with a partner or small group and write your plan in the space that follows before transferring to presentation media of your choice. If necessary, continue writing your plan on a separate sheet of paper and attach it to this activity sheet.

List intelligence: _____   *Cinderella Wants to Go to the Ball*

Lesson title: _____

Goals/Outcomes: *The students will be able to* _____

_____

_____

The Opportunity for a Solution: Cinderella wants to attend the ball but she does not have money or time to prepare herself. Without a fairy godmother, what other ways can Cinderella attend the ball?

Learning Activities: _____

_____

_____

_____

_____

Part 2: Present the lesson in a brief synopsis using the board, poster paper, or digital projection to share and explain your lesson plan.

Part 3: Once all lessons have been shared, work together with the class to combine different activities that could reach multiple intelligences in one lesson plan!

Gifted and Talented or ELL Opportunities

Activity D   **Name** _____ **Date** _____ **Period** _____

Part 1: Consider the information in the text regarding students who are gifted and talented or students with limited English proficiency. Then research your own school and your community to determine what is being done locally to assist the development of such students. Write your responses to the following to guide your research for creating a public-service publication.

1. Research online to learn as much as you can about the offerings at your school. Cite your sources for further reference and note details in the space provided.

    _____

    _____

    _____

    _____

    _____

    _____

2. Determine how many students are impacted by the programs offered and how the school district identifies these students.

    _____

    _____

    _____

    _____

    _____

3. When are the opportunities available to students? during the normal school day? Do these opportunities take them away from other learning? Why or why not?

    _____

    _____

    _____

    _____

4. What are the qualifications of the leaders for these programs? What sort of special training do they need/have?

    _____

    _____

    _____

5. How is information about students communicated to home and within the school?

    _____

    _____

    _____

    _____

(Continued)

6. How are students evaluated and how often?

_____

_____

_____

7. What is the community impact of the program?

_____

_____

_____

_____

_____

8. Additional questions or information.

_____

_____

_____

_____

_____

Part 2: Now that you have completed your research, create a visual that provides clear, detailed information about programs for exceptional children and students with limited English proficiency in your community. Your goal is to create either hard-copy handouts like fliers and brochures or digital media that can be displayed and accessed electronically. Your focus is to *inform* the community audience the options available to assist these students in your school.

Part 3: After creating your publication, present it to the class. Then use the following rubric to self-assess. For each category in the rubric, place a check (✓) in the box that you think best represents your performance on this project *(Exceeds Expectations, Meets Expectations, Developing, Needs Improvement)*. Then write a brief summary on each section following the rubric regarding your development and level of work provided in each category.

Categories	Exceeds Expectations	Meets Expectations	Developing	Needs Improvement
Research *(Demonstrated in format of your choice)* 3 sources/1 personal contact Citations for research Personal contact interview write-up Background information Complete Well written	15–14	13–12	11–9	8–0

(Continued)

Categories	Exceeds Expectations	Meets Expectations	Developing	Needs Improvement
Digital Display or Hard Copy 10 or more facts regarding program Strong focus on topic Quality design Visuals are used to enhance information	20–18	17–15	14–13	12–0
Time Management Used class time effectively Progress at check-in On time	10	9–8	7–5	4–0
Project Appearance Neat Free from errors Creative	10–9	8–7	6	5–0
Class Presentation (optional) Knowledge of content Logical progression of information	15–14	13–12	11–9	8–0

1. Research: _____

_____

_____

_____

_____

_____

2. Digital display or hard copy flyer or brochure: _____

_____

_____

_____

_____

_____

(Continued)

Name _____

3. Time management: _____
   _____
   _____
   _____
   _____
   _____
   _____
   _____
   _____

4. Project appearance: _____
   _____
   _____
   _____
   _____
   _____
   _____
   _____
   _____

5. Class presentation: _____
   _____
   _____
   _____
   _____
   _____
   _____
   _____
   _____

Interview or Observe a Special Education Professional

Activity E   **Name** _____ **Date** _____ **Period** _____

Complete the following form as you observe or interview a special education professional. If necessary, continue your responses on a separate sheet of paper and attach it to this activity sheet.

Name of Professional: _____   **Length of Visit:** _____

Number of Students Impacted: _____   **Signature of Professional** _____

1. Special features of the classroom: _____

   _____

   _____

   _____

   _____

   _____

2. How is teaching in this type of situation different from teaching in a regular classroom?

   _____

   _____

   _____

3. How many classes/students does this specialist see each day? How long is each class?

   _____

   _____

   _____

4. Why is this class enjoyable to teach? _____

   _____

5. What are some challenges to teaching this course compared to the class in which you are currently an intern?

   _____

   _____

   _____

6. What set curriculum requirements, if any, must this specialist meet for the year? _____

   _____

   _____

   _____

7. Additional observations. _____

   _____

   _____

   _____

Chapter 10
What Makes an Effective Teacher?

Building Your Pedagogical Vocabulary

Activity A   Name _____   Date _____   Period _____

As you read through Chapter 10 of the *Teaching* text, identify the vocabulary terms in the following chart. With your partner, you must:

- **A.** Choose and define the term
- **B.** Explain its value in the teaching profession
- **C.** Create a flash card on an 8½- by 11-inch sheet of paper with the *term*, *definition*, and *value*

You have 15 minutes to complete this task. Once time is up, post your flash card on the board. Then take a *gallery walk*—a tour past the posted class work for reviewing and learning—to view all the flash cards and record the definitions and values in the chart that follows.

Facilitator *Definition:* *Value to teaching:*	**Direct learning** *Definition:* *Value to teaching:*
Teachable moment *Definition:* *Value to teaching:*	**Assessment** *Definition:* *Value to teaching:*
Mission statement *Definition:* *Value to teaching:*	**Lifelong learner** *Definition:* *Value to teaching:*
Professional development *Definition:* *Value to teaching:*	**Mixed message** *Definition:* *Value to teaching:*

(Continued)

Active listening	**Assertive communicator**
Definition:	*Definition:*
Value to teaching:	*Value to teaching:*
Aggressive communicator	**Passive communicator**
Definition:	*Definition:*
Value to teaching:	*Value to teaching:*
Mediator	**Mediation**
Definition:	*Definition:*
Value to teaching:	*Value to teaching:*
Ethics	**Collaboration**
Definition:	*Definition:*
Value to teaching:	*Value to teaching:*
Optimism	**Proactive**
Definition:	*Definition:*
Value to teaching:	*Value to teaching:*
Organizational culture	**Intangible**
Definition:	*Definition:*
Value to teaching:	*Value to teaching:*
Chain of command	**Heimlich Maneuver (abdominal thrust)**
Definition:	*Definition:*
Value to teaching:	*Value to teaching:*

Teachers as Facilitators

Activity B   **Name** _____   **Date** _____   **Period** _____

Throughout your day you are exposed to several different educators and a variety of teaching styles. Today, specifically watch for ways one of your teachers guides the learning process. Choose a teacher you know does an excellent job, and ask them ahead of time if it is acceptable for you to record some comments while actively engaging in the lesson. Explain your assignment and show them this form. Write your responses in the space that follows.

1. Briefly explain the format of the lesson (lecture, questioning, discussion, individual or group work, etc.).

   _____

   _____

   _____

   _____

   _____

2. Explain examples of facilitated learning you see. _____

   _____

   _____

   _____

   _____

   _____

3. Explain examples of direct learning you observe. _____

   _____

   _____

   _____

   _____

4. List an open-ended question the teacher used during this class. Explain how the students responded.

   _____

   _____

   _____

   _____

5. Did you observe a teachable moment? Summarize the event and how the students responded.

   _____

   _____

   _____

   _____

   _____

Grading and Evaluating Student Growth

Name _____   **Date** _____   **Period** _____

Answer the questions that follow as you interview your cooperating teacher about his or her grading methods, evaluation policies, and procedures.

Optional assignment: (A) Type your responses as a paper. (B) Use your responses to create a visual highlighting the best practices in grading and assessment.

1. What standards (local, state, national, common core, etc.) do you use to guide your assessments?

   _____

   _____

   _____

   _____

   _____

2. What is the difference between *formative* and *summative* assessments? _____

   _____

   _____

   _____

   _____

   _____

3. How do you use both *formative* and *summative* assessments? _____

   _____

   _____

   _____

   _____

   _____

4. How do you use these assessments to improve student learning? _____

   _____

   _____

   _____

   _____

   _____

5. What process do you use to assign grades or benchmark achievement? _____

   _____

   _____

   _____

   _____

   _____

(Continued)

6. How much time do you spend grading? How do you communicate your grading policies to students and their guardians?

_____

_____

_____

_____

_____

_____

7. Do you ever grade participation? If so, how do you see this benefiting the students?

_____

_____

_____

_____

_____

_____

8. Do you ever encounter or use a *Pass/Fail* grading system? If so, please explain.

_____

_____

_____

_____

_____

_____

9. Describe a time when a student or parent disagreed with your grading policies and how you handled it.

_____

_____

_____

_____

_____

10. How do the assessments students complete impact your rating as an educator? What are your thoughts on this dynamic?

_____

_____

_____

_____

_____

_____

Teacher Ethics

Activity D   **Name** _____   **Date** _____   **Period** _____

Part 1: Choose one of the scenarios that follow, read it, and then answer the questions that follow. (*Note:* Some questions may not apply to your chosen scenario.)

A. A teacher regularly works with students through an after school club she sponsors. Over time, she has given students her personal phone number to expedite communication during events. Occasionally, students will text their teacher personal concerns and questions.

B. During a small group activity, the teacher overhears students talking about smoking marijuana in detail.

C. The teacher overhears an ELL student say that his parents have returned to China. They plan to come back in a month. They taught him to pay all the bills and how to shop for groceries.

D. A student seems to be doing well in class; all of his papers are well written and precise. However, he never turns in his homework and is frequently off-task in class. The teacher, Mr. Smith, wonders if he is boring this student. Is the students level that much higher? Mr. Smith investigates how the student is doing in other classes so he can get some ideas from other teachers. The student is doing poorly in all his academic classes except Mr. Smith's. Mr. Smith discusses it with his supervisor, and finds out that the student's older brother was a *straight A* student and took the same course two years ago. It appears he may be using his brother's papers.

E. Mrs. Jones is spending her spring break at the beach with friends and family. The house she is staying at is next door to a family whose children attend the same school at which she teaches. Mrs. Jones wears a bikini when she is at the beach and partakes in an alcoholic beverage occasionally.

F. Miss Ames is doing her student teaching at a school near her family's house. She has one student in particular who displays erratic off-task behavior, is frequently inappropriate, and struggles academically. Miss Ames is frustrated and decides to talk to her neighbor, a former teacher, about the situation. She uses the student's name and specifically describes the concerns.

G. Each day once school lets out, Mr. Farraj sits at his desk to grade papers and organize for the next day. His window is open most days and he can see the students exiting the school. One day he hears some students discussing the physical characteristics of another student. They are talking about taking pictures of the student during class and posting them to an Internet site.

1. What scenario did you read (insert letter)? _____

2. What problems might this scenario raise? _____

_____

_____

_____

_____

_____

3. In what ways may the law, ethical code, or other school policies be violated? _____

_____

_____

_____

_____

_____

_____

(Continued)

4. What do you do about this situation as a teacher? Outline your plan. _____

_____

_____

_____

_____

_____

_____

5. What are some possible negative consequences for the teacher, or students, and the school? _____

_____

_____

_____

_____

_____

_____

6. What is a positive outcome of this situation? _____

_____

_____

_____

_____

_____

_____

7. What are the repercussions of inaction? _____

_____

_____

_____

_____

_____

_____

Part 2: Complete one of the following options after answering the preceding questions.

    A. Discuss the scenario in a small group and report back to the class.

    B. Discuss the scenario with your cooperating teacher and how he/she would respond.

Examining Mission and Vision

Activity E   **Name** _____   **Date** _____   **Period** _____

Use online or print resources to look up the mission and vision statement for your school or district or one of a neighboring school system. Review the statement and answer the questions that follow.

1. Which school did you look up and where did you find their mission and vision statement? _____

   _____

   _____

   _____

   _____

   _____

   _____

2. What is the actual purpose of the statement? _____

   _____

   _____

   _____

   _____

   _____

   _____

3. What are the goals of the statement? _____

   _____

   _____

   _____

   _____

   _____

   _____

4. How do you envision the school environment based on the statement? _____

   _____

   _____

   _____

   _____

   _____

5. If this statement is for your own school, how do you see the mission or vision in action? _____

   _____

   _____

   _____

   _____

   _____

Effective Communication

Many times as a teacher you will find yourself communicating with parents through e-mail. Read the following e-mail message from a high school parent. Then write how you would respond in the space provided.

> *Dear Mr. Anderson,*
>
> *Sarah would be very upset if she knew I was communicating with you about her final grade. Her Dad took her away for the weekend and I just took a look at her grades. To be honest with you, she does need the A—I understand the position you are in. It seems so desperate to have her grade point hinge on two percent of a grade. The big picture, however, is that she has applied to a university (her dream school) and the school is waiting to see her first semester grades for this year. She did poorly during freshmen and sophomore years and is paying a heavy price this year. I do understand, by her own admission, that she crossed the line with you a few times. I am sorry about this. If there is anything you can do—participation points? Extra Credit? Please let me know.*
>
> *Sincerely,*
>
> *Sarah's Mom, Mrs. Flesher*

_____

_____

_____

_____

_____

_____

_____

_____

_____

_____

_____

_____

_____

_____

_____

_____

_____

_____

_____

_____

Conflict Resolution

Activity G   Name _____   Date _____   Period _____

Part 1: Every day thousands of conflicts arise within the school environment. Teaching students and adults to resolve those conflicts through constructive resolution is essential in any educational environment. In a small group, brainstorm a variety of conflicts you have seen within the classrooms in which you are interns. Choose one of these scenarios, without identifying specific students, and write a script in the space provided for a brief skit demonstrating the conflict and how it could have been resolved through the conflict-resolution steps outlined in the text.

1. Explain the conflict. _____

    _____

    _____

    _____

    _____

2. Describe how you would resolve it using each of these steps:

    - Clarify the issue.

        _____

        _____

    - Find out what each person wants.

        _____

        _____

    - Identify various alternatives.

        _____

        _____

    - Decide how to negotiate.

        _____

        _____

    - Choose the best alternative.

        _____

        _____

    - Solidify the agreement.

        _____

        _____

    - Review and renegotiate if necessary.

        _____

        _____

Part 2: Present your skit to the class. Discuss with the class whether this conflict-resolution strategy was successful.

Chapter 11
Planning for Instruction

Building Your Pedagogical Vocabulary

Activity A   Name _____   Date _____   Period _____

Part 1: Choose one or more important terms from this chapter. Do the following:

    A. Define the term(s)

    B. Provide an example of the word(s) in context

    C. Supply a visual representation of the term

You will have 15 minutes to complete this task and then present your term or terms to the class.

Part 2: While others are presenting, write their definitions, context that makes sense to you, and describe their visuals in the space provided.

Term	Definition	Context	Visual
Educational standards			
Curriculum development			
Course plan			
Instructional units			
Lesson plans			
Instructional objectives			

(Continued)

Bloom's Taxonomy			
Learning activities			
Assessment			
Transitions			
Guided practice			
Independent practice			
Controversy			
Formulaic			
Viable			
Energizer (look up online, not in text)			
Icebreaker (look up online, not in text)			

Icebreakers, Energizers, and Transitions

Activity B **Name** _____ **Date** _____ **Period** _____

Icebreakers and *energizers* are intended to be quick (five minutes or less), transitional activities that get children moving, laughing, and comfortable. Icebreakers may help students know each other better and increase level of comfort. Energizers may be used to stimulate enthusiasm or transition to refocus students. *Transitions* are sometimes used to prepare students for a new activity or lesson.

Part 1: Search online for one *icebreaker* activity, one *energizer* activity, and one *transition* activity suitable for children in the grade in which you are interning. To avoid duplication of activities, select activities that you have not seen used before in the classroom. Record the details as follows about each activity in the space provided for each activity type.

Icebreaker

Activity title: _____

Activity source (URL, etc.): _____

Target grade level for activity: _____

Materials needed (if any): _____

Directions for facilitating or executing activity: _____

_____

_____

_____

_____

_____

_____

_____

_____

Energizer

Activity title: _____

Activity source (URL, etc.): _____

Target grade level for activity: _____

Materials needed (if any): _____

Directions for facilitating or executing activity: _____

_____

_____

_____

_____

_____

_____

_____

(Continued)

Transition

Activity title: _____

Activity source (URL, etc.): _____

Target grade level for activity: _____

Materials needed (if any): _____

Directions for facilitating or executing activity: _____

_____

_____

_____

_____

_____

_____

_____

_____

_____

Part 2: Present one of your three activities to the class. Your activity should take approximately 5 minutes or less. You are responsible for bringing in the needed materials, although it is permissible to ask if your teacher has any of them available.

Part 3: As your peers lead you in icebreakers, energizers, and transitions, record one of each that you would like to use in your classroom. Write your responses in the space provided.

1. **Icebreaker name:** _____

2. Grade level to use with: _____

3. Directions to facilitate or execute: _____

   _____

   _____

   _____

   _____

   _____

   _____

   _____

   _____

4. Modifications I might make for students who have special needs: _____

   _____

   _____

   _____

5. **Energizer name:** _____

(Continued)

Name _____

6. Grade Level to use with: _____

7. Directions to facilitate or execute: _____

_____

_____

_____

_____

_____

_____

_____

_____

_____

8. Modifications I might make for students who have special needs: _____

_____

_____

_____

_____

_____

_____

9. **Transition name:** _____

10. Grade Level to use with: _____

11. Directions to facilitate or execute: _____

_____

_____

_____

_____

_____

_____

_____

_____

12. Modifications I might make for students who have special needs: _____

_____

_____

_____

_____

_____

Recognizing Effective Teaching

Activity C   **Name** _____   **Date** _____   **Period** _____

Observe your cooperating teacher during an entire class lesson. You may observe another teacher if necessary. Identify the various parts of the lesson you observe.

School: _____

Teacher: _____   **Grade:** _____

1. What is the objective of the lesson? How was this communicated to the students? _____
   _____
   _____
   _____
   _____

2. What equipment and materials did the lesson require? _____
   _____
   _____
   _____
   _____

3. How does the teacher focus the students on the lesson? _____
   _____
   _____
   _____
   _____

4. What instructional strategies did the teacher use to deliver the lesson? _____
   _____
   _____
   _____
   _____

5. How is the lesson organized? Write out the sequence of events. _____
   _____
   _____
   _____
   _____

6. How did the teacher check for understanding? _____
   _____
   _____
   _____
   _____

(Continued)

7. How were the students engaged? Was there guided practice/independent practice?

_____

_____

_____

_____

8. How does closure take place? How does it relate back to the objective? _____

_____

_____

_____

9. Were any of the following techniques used, and if so, how? Give specific examples.

   Anticipatory Set or Hook (a way to get students interested!):

_____

_____

_____

   Wait Time (giving students a period of time to formulate an answer):

_____

_____

_____

   Teachable Moment(s):

_____

_____

_____

10. How does the teacher incorporate lesson components that appeal to each of the learning styles?

    Visual:

_____

_____

_____

    Auditory:

_____

_____

_____

    Kinesthetic:

_____

_____

_____

Curriculum Development

Activity D   **Name** _____   **Date** _____   **Period** _____

Part 1: Choose one of the current initiatives highlighted in the text. Research the background, projected impact on student learning and achievement, and the current outcomes of the initiative. Record the information and your sources in the space that follows.

Common Core State Standards (CCSS)

Science, Technology, Engineering, (Art) and Math (STEM or STEAM)

Next Generation Science Standards (NCGS)

Chosen initiative: _____

1. History or background: _____

   _____

   _____

   _____

   _____

   _____

   Source: _____

2. Important dates in development and implementation: _____

   _____

   _____

   _____

   _____

   Source: _____

3. Projected impact on student learning and achievement: _____

   _____

   _____

   _____

   _____

   Source: _____

4. Current outcomes of the initiative: _____

   _____

   _____

   _____

   _____

   _____

   Source: _____

(Continued)

Name _____

5. Opposing viewpoints: _____

_____

_____

_____

_____

_____

_____

_____

_____

_____

Source(s): _____

_____

Part 2: Form a small group with others who have completed research on the same initiative. Discuss the preceding information and compare and contrast your findings. Confirm your understanding is correct. Create a visually appealing poster to highlight the important information regarding that initiative. Use the space that follows to sketch or describe a plan what the poster will look like. *Option:* Create a photo essay or digital poster.

How to Organize Learning

Your teacher will explain to you how he or she plans out the course in which you are currently enrolled. Use the space that follows to take notes regarding his or her course planning.

1. How do class schedules differ between your school and the school at which you intern? _____

_____

_____

_____

_____

_____

2. How do class/school schedules impact planning? _____

_____

_____

_____

_____

_____

_____

_____

3. What student characteristic may impact planning? _____

_____

_____

_____

_____

_____

_____

_____

4. List the instructional units in this course. _____

_____

_____

_____

_____

_____

_____

_____

_____

(Continued)

5. What outside opportunities for learning does the teacher incorporate? _____

_____

_____

_____

_____

_____

_____

6. How do the teacher's personal characteristics impact the course? _____

_____

_____

_____

_____

_____

7. When and how does the teacher create lesson plans for the course? _____

_____

_____

_____

_____

_____

_____

8. Who is involved in the lesson planning process? Are lesson plans turned in to anyone for review?

_____

_____

_____

_____

9. Who benefits from having lesson plans? How? _____

_____

_____

_____

_____

_____

Lesson Planning

Activity F **Name** _____ **Date** _____ **Period** _____

Part 1: Work with your cooperating teacher to come up with a lesson you can teach to the students during your placement. Use the following form to prepare to write the lesson plan and teach the lesson.

1. Ask the teacher to describe how he or she would teach the lesson. What instructional strategies are used?

   _____

   _____

   _____

   _____

2. Does he or she want you to teach the lesson in the same format or is there some flexibility or a component that he or she wants to improve?

   _____

   _____

   _____

   _____

3. What resources are available to you to prepare you for the lesson? _____

   _____

   _____

   _____

   _____

4. How will learning be assessed? _____

   _____

   _____

   _____

5. How long will the lesson need to be and when will you teach it? _____

   _____

   _____

   _____

6. What prior knowledge will students have from previous lessons and what knowledge will they need to have to be successful in the lesson you will present?

   _____

   _____

   _____

7. What accommodations or modifications need to be made for students? _____

   _____

   _____

   _____

(Continued)

Name _____

Part 2: Now use the information you have gathered and the details in the text. Create a lesson plan using the following format. Once you complete the following form, type it up and ask your cooperating teacher to review it and approve it with his or her signature before you teach the lesson.

- Revise the plan in any way your teacher suggests.

- Provide your cooperating teacher with the feedback form to complete during your lesson.

Lesson Plan Guide

Intern Name: _____

School: _____

Co-op teacher approval signature: _____

The target objectives for the intern are to:

- Effectively communicate with cooperating teacher.

- Understand the process of constructing a lesson plan and concepts to be taught.

- Implement **new** instructional strategies and materials to facilitate student learning.

- Maintain student attention and cooperation while teaching a lesson plan.

Date of Lesson:	Subject:	Grade Level:
General Unit of Study	Name of unit:	
Day's Lesson Concept/Topic	Name of lesson concept or topic:	
Learner Characteristics	Number of students: Age(s): Boys: Girls: Special needs: Behavior issues:	
Specific Objectives What are two or three main things you want students to learn from your lesson? Written objectives should be *measurable* and follow Bloom's taxonomy. Use the phrase, "Students will be able to" and then begin the objective with verb from Bloom's Taxonomy followed by objective.	*Students will be able to* • _____ _____ • _____ _____ • _____ _____ • _____ _____ How will you link the new materials to prior learning? _____ _____	

(Continued)

Lesson Plan Guide	
Time Period	
Introduction (Hook)	How will you engage the students right away?
Step-by-Step Procedures (Details including instructional strategies you will use and timing.) • Introduction/transitions • Teacher talking • Questioning • Student interactions • Individual seat work • Small group work • Activity • Lesson closure	
Summary (Closure)	How will you summarize and check for understanding?
Assessment	How will you assess student growth and learning?
Instructional Materials and Equipment	What materials will you use to teach the lesson?
Adaptations for Students Who Have Special Needs	
Learning Styles to Address	How are you addressing all three learning styles in this lesson?
Notes	

(Continued)

Name _____

Co-op Teacher—Lesson Planning and Teaching Feedback Form

Intern Name _____   School _____

Date of Lesson:	Subject:	Grade Level:
Day's Lesson Concept:		
Targets	**Cooperating Teacher Feedback**	
Ability to collaborate on the lesson plan with cooperating teacher		
Level of understanding the process of constructing a lesson plan		
Level of planning and preparation for lesson		
Level of understanding of content objectives		
Level of comfort in teacher role		
Ability to maintain eye contact and student's attention		
Ability to effectively sequence the lesson		
Ability to effectively time each activity		
Ability to implement existing instructional strategies and materials to teach lesson		

What suggestions do you have to help your intern improve?

1.

2.

Additional Comments:

Cooperating teacher a signature _____   **Date** _____

Evaluating Your Effectiveness after Teaching the Lesson

Activity G   **Name** _____   **Date** _____   **Period** _____

Complete the following self-evaluation after you have presented your lesson. Write your responses in the space provided.

Targets	Student Reflection
Ability to collaborate on the lesson plan with cooperating teacher	
Level of understanding the process of constructing a lesson plan	
Level of planning and preparation for lesson	
Level of understanding of content objectives	
Level of comfort in teacher role	
Ability to maintain eye contact and student's attention	
Ability to effectively sequence the lesson	
Ability to effectively time each activity	
Ability to implement existing instructional strategies and materials to teach lesson	
What three targets would you most like to improve?	**What can you, your cooperating teacher, or your classroom teacher do to help you improve those characteristics?**
1.	1.
2.	2.
3.	3.

Once you have completed this evaluation, meet with your cooperating teacher and discuss your responses and his or her responses regarding your performance. If necessary, continue your comments on a separate sheet of paper and attach it to this activity sheet.

Intern signature _____   **Date** _____

Chapter 12
Instructional Methods

Visual Vocabulary

Activity A   Name _____   Date _____   Period _____

Part 1: Write the definition of each term in your own words in the chart below. Look for pictures or video clips that demonstrate the term and cite your sources in the space provided.

Term	My Definition	Picture/Clip to Represent URL of image or video clip
Instructional method		
Critical thinking		
Open-ended questioning		
Wait time		
Pacing		
Closure		
Teacher-centered		
Learner-centered		
Panel discussion		
Simulation		

(Continued)

Term	My Definition	Picture/Clip to Represent URL of image or video clip
Skit		
Role-playing		
Case study		
Reflective response		
Productive lab		
Experimental lab		
Cooperative learning		
Individual accountability		
Collaborative learning		
Differentiated instructional method		
Repertoire		
Moderator		
Consensus		
Empower		

Part 2: Choose one of the following options and create a visual that demonstrates each of the academic terms in the above chart. Share your visual-vocabulary project with the class.

    A. Develop a video montage by using the software of your choice to string together video clips of each term being demonstrated.

    B. Create a collage with pictures from magazines or printed from the Internet that demonstrate each term.

Learning About Teaching Strategies

Activity B   Name _____   Date _____   Period _____

Complete the following chart for each of the teaching techniques listed. Explain each technique, determine if it is learner- or teacher-centered, identify the benefits and shortcomings (if any) of the technique.

Technique	Explanation	Learner- or Teacher-Centered	Benefits of This Technique	Shortcomings of This Technique
Lectures				
Reading				
Discussions				
Demonstrations				
Guest speakers				
Simulations				
Skits				

Technique	Explanation	Learner- or Teacher-Centered	Benefits of This Technique	Shortcomings of This Technique
Role-playing				
Case studies				
Reflective responses				
Labs				
Games				
Student presentations				
Cooperative learning				
Collaborative learning				

Arranging for a Guest Speaker

Activity C   **Name** _____   **Date** _____   **Period** _____

Guest speakers who have special knowledge or experience with a topic or subject pertinent to a class you are teaching can be a wonderful asset to enhancing and supplementing class curriculum. As you begin to plan for a guest speaker, it is important to consider the following questions:

- How can a guest speaker help educate students on a topic?
- How does the speaker relate to curriculum that is already in place for the class?
- What do you anticipate students will gain from the guest speaker?
- Who are some possible guest speakers you can contact on the topic?

Part 1: Your first task will be to discuss the guest-speaker project with your cooperating teacher and complete the following proposal form. Allow yourself plenty of time to coordinate the speaker as you may need to approach several potential speakers before one agrees. Review the *expectations* for the project prior to starting the assignment. After talking with your cooperating teacher, complete the items that follow:

1. Potential topics for a guest speaker: _____

   _____

   _____

2. Possible dates that work with the class schedule: _____

   _____

   _____

3. Possible audience for the speaker in addition to your class: _____

   _____

   _____

4. Space available for the speaker's presentation: _____

   _____

   _____

5. Funding arrangements (if necessary): _____

   _____

   _____

Expectations for the Guest-Speaker Project
Target objectives of the guest-speaker project are to:
• Understand the process of arranging and facilitating a guest speaker.
• Match the content of ongoing curriculum with the content presented by the guest speaker.
• Understand the process of effective communication among the guest speaker, the parents/guardians, the school, the cooperating teacher, and the students.
• Reflect on the effectiveness of the guest speaker.
Your grade is based on (note artifacts required as deliverables):

(Continued)

Expectations for the Guest-Speaker Project
• Evidence of understanding of target objectives (10 points)
• Proper completion of Activity C/ *Guest-Speaker Proposal* form (5 points)
• Effective communication with all parties (cooperating teacher, guest speaker, principal, parents/guardians, students, and others; includes copies of all correspondence and signatures from cooperating teacher and principal (if required) (25 points)
• Depth of question responses for reflection questions (30 points)
• Photographs of guest speaker only (no student faces; minimum of 10 photographs) (5 points)
• Self-assessment rubric (10 points)
• Cooperating teacher awards points for professionalism and communication (15 points)
• **Total project points** = 100
Items to turn in for this project:
• This activity sheet (Activity C) which contains the following: *Guest-Speaker Proposal*, drafts of correspondence, your answers to reflection questions, and the self-assessment rubric
• Copies of all additional correspondence or written documentation of conversations (guest speaker, cooperating teacher, principal, parents/guardians, students, and others)
• Photographs of guest speaker during presentation
• Copies of thank-you notes to speaker (yours and the students)

Part 2: In the space that follows, brainstorm at least five possible guest speakers who could speak to one of the topics discussed with your cooperating teacher. Write your ideas in the space that follows. Choose one speaker and then complete the *Guest-Speaker Proposal* form and acquire your cooperating teacher's signature.

(Continued)

Name _____

Guest-Speaker Proposal

Topic Speaker will address: _____

Proposed Date of Speaker: _____

Name of Speaker: _____

Qualifications of Speaker: _____

The student intern has discussed with me the requirements of facilitating a guest speaker. I understand that the intern may reserve a speaker that has been used in previous years. The intern, however, is responsible for all the details regarding planning, presentation, and follow-up for the speaker.

Cooperating teacher signature: _____ Date: _____

Part 3: In the space that follows, write an initial draft of a letter or e-mail message to the guest speaker. Ask if the speaker is available to speak with your class, noting the content the speaker is to cover, date and day, and location (address and room number). Be sure to ask the speaker if he or she has any needs (handouts to be printed; audio-visual equipment needs, etc.) or questions about the speaking engagement. Make sure your letter or e-mail message is written clearly using correct grammar and spelling. Keep copies of all correspondence with the speaker to turn in with this assignment.

Dear _____

_____

_____

_____

_____

_____

_____

_____

_____

_____

_____

Part 4: Talk with your cooperating teacher about any special needs your speaker has for the speaking engagement (audio-visual, photocopying handouts, etc.) and make arrangements for these items. In addition, inform the school principal or administrator about your guest speaker, and note any special requirements for escorting the speaker to your class.

6. Handout preparation needs: _____

_____

7. Audio-visual needs: _____

_____

8. Date school principal was informed about the speaker: _____

Principal's signature (if necessary): _____

(Continued)

Part 5: After your initial contact, write and send a follow-up letter or e-mail message (or have a conversation with the speaker) confirming the plans for the speaking engagement with the speaker. Note the topic, date, time, and location. Ensure the speaker that you have made arrangements for any audio-visual equipment and preparation of any handouts the speaker will need. Be sure to thank the speaker for agreeing to speak to your class. Draft a copy of your message in the following space.

Dear _____

_____

_____

_____

_____

_____

_____

_____

Part 6: Write a newsletter article, letter, or e-mail message to the parents or guardians of your students to inform them about the guest speaker. Draft a copy of your newsletter article or message in the space that follows. Be sure to include the speaker's name and topic, date, time, and location of the presentation. Inform the parents that your cooperating teacher is aware of the speaker and is in agreement with the presentation.

_____

_____

_____

_____

_____

_____

_____

_____

Part 7: Inform your students that they will be having a guest speaker and indicate the topic on which he or she will be speaking. Note the date, day, and time on the board. Have each student write three questions he or she has for the speaker. Collect the questions and combine them into one list to have available to the speaker on the day of the engagement. Attach the compiled list of questions to this activity project sheet.

Part 8: Two to three days prior to the speaking engagement, do the following tasks. Obtain signatures as necessary in the space provided.

9. Contact your guest speaker and confirm all arrangements and approval of visuals. Note the date of correspondence and attach a copy of the message to this activity.

_____

10. Review all plans with your cooperating teacher. Note the date and time of this conversation: _____

_____

(Continued)

11. Notify the school office about the date and time your guest speaker will arrive so the staff can escort or direct the speaker to the correct location.

   Signature of office staff (if necessary): _____

12. Finalize arrangements for the space to accommodate your speaker, students, and the presentation.

13. Prepare your students for the guest speaker's presentation. Convey behavior expectations of the students during the presentation. Provide any additional background information students need prior to the presentation. Review initial questions students prepared and have students add any others to the list.

14. Copy handouts for the speaker and confirm arrangements for audio-visual equipment.

   Signature of cooperating teacher confirming completion of items 12, 13, and 14:

   _____

Part 9: The day of your guest speaker's presentation has arrived. You are likely feeling excited (and perhaps a little anxious) about the presentation. Remember to smile as you do the following:

- **Greet** your guest speaker (if possible) and escort him or her to the speaking location.
- **Allow** a few minutes for your speaker to set up and get acclimated to the location.
- **Introduce** the guest speaker to your cooperating teacher and the students.
- **Take** photographs of the guest speaker throughout the presentation (omitting student faces)
- **Position** yourself in the room so you can monitor student behavior and model appropriate attention to the speaker.
- **Signal** your guest speaker when it is time for student questions.
- **Lead** the students in saying "thank you" to the speaker.

Part 10: Write your responses to the following questions in the space provided to reflect on your guest-speaker project based on the target objectives identified in *Part 1* of this assignment.

15. Understand the process of arranging and facilitating a guest-speaker:

   a. What was the process you went through to arrange for and facilitate the guest-speaker project?

   _____

   _____

   _____

   _____

   b. What was the process you went through with the school in making arrangements for the guest speaker?

   _____

   _____

   _____

   _____

   c. How did you address the cost of having a guest speaker, if there was one?

   _____

   _____

   _____

   _____

(Continued)

16. Match the content of ongoing curriculum with the content presented by the guest speaker.

    a. What was the unit of study? _____

    _____

    b. Where does the guest speaker fit in to the unit? _____

    _____

    c. How did the guest speaker facilitate greater understanding of the unit? _____

    _____

    _____

    d. How did you incorporate the guest speaker's presentation in the follow-up lesson (if required)? _____

    _____

    _____

17. Match the content of ongoing curriculum with the content presented by the guest speaker.

    a. How did you communicate with the parents/guardians regarding the guest speaker? _____

    _____

    _____

    b. How did you communicate with the guest speaker, prior to, during and after the engagement? _____

    _____

    _____

    c. How did you involve the cooperating teacher in the guest-speaker project? _____

    _____

    _____

    d. How did you involve the students in thanking the guest-speaker? _____

    _____

    _____

18. Reflect on the effectiveness of the guest speaker.

    a. How did you involve students in question formation? _____

    _____

    _____

    b. How did the students respond to the guest speaker? _____

    _____

    _____

    c. What went well? What didn't? _____

    _____

    _____

    d. Reflect on this assignment—give concrete feedback about your experience. _____

    _____

    _____

(Continued)

Name _____

Self-Assessment—Guest-Speaker Project				
Guest speaker name:				
Project Parts	**Points Possible**	**Your Comments**		**Points Earned**
Evidence of understanding of target objectives as noted by proper completion of this activity • Completion of self-assessment	10			
Proper completion of Activity C / proposal form: • Submitted on time • Complete, including how you chose this unit for a speaker	10			
Effective Communication: • Reservation process for guest speaker including names and contact information • Copy of confirmation letters/e-mails or communication log • Parent notification via newsletter, letter, or e-mail (or copy of correspondence created even if not used) • Thank-you notes for speaker	25			
Depth of answers to reflection questions: • Answers all of the questions indicated influence and process of arranging, reflection on what you have learned and what the students responses were, details of the unit of study, where the speaker falls in it, summary, prearranged student questions, etc.	35			
Pictures of guest speaker(s) and of their activities or visuals • Minimum of 10 photos • No student faces showing	5			
Cooperating teacher grade • Communications and accountability • Professionalism in overall completion of project	15			
Total points awarded (100 possible):				

(Continued)

Cooperating Teacher Assessment—Guest-Speaker Project

Guest speaker name:

Project Parts	Points Possible	Your Comments	Points Earned
Evidence of understanding of target objectives as noted by proper completion of this activity • Completion of self-assessment	10		
Proper completion of Activity C /proposal form: • Submitted on time • Complete, including how you chose this unit for a speaker	10		
Effective Communication: • Reservation process for guest speaker including names and contact information • Copy of confirmation letters/e-mails or communication log • Parent notification via newsletter, letter, or e-mail (or copy of correspondence created even if not used) • Thank-you notes for speaker	25		
Depth of answers to reflection questions: • Answers all of the questions indicated influence and process of arranging, reflection on what you have learned and what the students responses were, details of the unit of study, where the speaker falls in it, summary, prearranged student questions, etc.	35		
Pictures of guest speaker(s) and of their activities or visuals • Minimum of 10 photos • No student faces showing	5		
Cooperating teacher grade • Communications and accountability • Professionalism in overall completion of project	15		
Total points awarded (100 possible):			

Creating Games for Instruction

Activity D   Name _____   Date _____   Period _____

As you learned in the text, games can be a useful way to reinforce learning and build skills. Talk with your cooperating teacher about an upcoming lesson or unit that requires reviewing content. Discuss different games you could use to review for the assessment for that unit. Then complete the following.

Part 1: Create a file-folder board game that will help students review for a unit assessment in a fun and interesting way! Use the following guidelines in creating your game.

1. List the topic or concept for your game: _____.

2. Gather materials: file folder(s), colored paper, and colored pencils or markers for creating the game board and question cards.

3. Label the file-folder tab with the name of your game.

4. Create enough questions and answers for the game to cover all the content for the lesson or unit topic. Incorporate the questions into playing the game using the game board. Develop question cards (about two inches by three inches) for all game questions and answers.

5. Develop the game board on the inside of the folder, making it neat, colorful, interesting, and creative. Relate the format of your game board and purpose of the game to the topic in some way. For example, for a lesson on water transportation your game board may look like a meandering river. Create a sketch of your game board in the space the follows:

6. Write directions for your game that make it perfectly clear how to play the game. Type the directions on a separate sheet of paper and glue them to the back cover of the file folder.

7. Make sure the content and difficulty of your game are age-appropriate for your students.

8. Take a picture or provide a digital copy of your game to your teacher for grading. Use the following rubric as a guide for developing your game.

9. Use the following self-assessment to evaluate your game once it is complete. For each category, place a check (✓) in the box identifying the number of points you think you earned for the category.

(Continued)

Game Design Rubric					
Name of game:					
Category	10 points	8 points	6 points	4 points	2 points
Design and Creativity	Game board is neat, creative, and colorful; following directions completely.	Game board is creative and colorful but some parts are a little messy.	Game board is missing one or two elements and could be neater.	Most directions were not followed and the board is messy.	Game board is finished but it is not colorful; lacks creativity.
Questions and Answers	All vocabulary terms, questions, and answers are well incorporated into the game.	Two vocabulary terms are missing or incorrect.	More than two terms are missing *or* the game is still playable answering most questions.	Half of the vocabulary terms are missing *or* few questions are used in the game.	Many terms are incorrect or missing and very few are required to play the game.
Format and Purpose	The purpose of the game relates directly to the topic and the game board represents the theme.	The purpose closely relates to the topic and the game board somewhat represents the theme.	The purpose partially relates to the topic but the game board does not clearly represent the theme.	The purpose slightly relates to the topic but does not represent the theme.	The purpose and theme of the game are unclear from the appearance of the board.
Directions	Directions make it perfectly clear how to play the game. They are neatly typed with minimal grammatical or spelling errors.	Directions are typed but have two to three minor grammatical errors. They are somewhat unclear or a step is missing.	There are more than three errors. Directions are unclear; two to three steps could be added for clarification.	Errors in spelling and grammar interfere with understanding of the game directions. Requires much revision.	Many steps are missing or incomplete. It is very difficult to understand how to play the game. Complete revision needed.
Content and Difficulty	Questions and rules of play are of an appropriate level—not too difficult and not too easy.	Rules of play are age appropriate but some questions are too easy or too difficult.	Game is a bit too simple for the grade level and some questions are too easy.	Game is very simple and most questions are too easily answered.	Game is not appropriate for the grade level and questions are too easy or too difficult.
Total points earned out of 50:					

Part 2—Optional: Design a review game in a digital format if you are experienced with coding. If not; consider other school-approved digital tools available to you and the students free of charge to create your game. Use the preceding rubric to evaluate your digital game as well.

Incorporating Instructional Methods

Activity E   Name _____   Date _____   Period _____

Part 1: Coordinate the opportunity to teach another lesson in your cooperating classroom. It may be a lesson using the game you designed, follow up to the guest speaker you arranged, or a lesson on another topic. Complete the lesson plan, paying special attention to the instructional methods you use and reflecting on your cooperating teachers' feedback from a prior lesson.

Lesson Plan		
Intern Name: _____		
School: _____		
Cooperating teacher approval signature _____		
Date of Lesson:	**Subject:**	**Grade Level:**
General Unit of Study	Name of unit:	
Day's Lesson Concept/Topic	Name of lesson concept or topic:	
Learner Characteristics	Number of students: Age(s): Boys: Girls: Special needs: Behavior issues:	
Specific Objectives What are two or three main things you want students to learn from your lesson? Written objectives should be *measurable* and follow Bloom's taxonomy. Use the phrase, "Students will be able to" and then begin the objective with verb from Bloom's Taxonomy followed by objective.	*Students will be able to* • _____ _____ • _____ _____ • _____ _____ • _____ _____ How will you link the new materials to prior learning? _____ _____	
Time Period		

(Continued)

Lesson Plan

Introduction (Hook)	How will you engage the students right away? _____ _____
Step-by-Step Procedures (Details including instructional strategies you will use and timing.) • Introduction/transitions • Teacher talking • Questioning • Student interactions • Individual seat work • Small group work • Activity • Lesson closure	_____ _____ _____ _____ _____ _____ _____ _____ _____ _____ _____ _____ _____
Summary (Closure)	How will you summarize and check for understanding? _____ _____
Assessment	How will you assess student growth and learning? _____ _____
Instructional Materials and Equipment	What materials will you use to teach the lesson? _____ _____
Adaptations for Students Who Have Special Needs	_____ _____
Learning Styles to Address	How are you addressing all three learning styles in this lesson? _____ _____
Notes	_____ _____

Cooperative teacher approval signature: _____

(Continued)

Name _____

Intern Name _____   School _____

Co-op Teacher—Lesson Planning and Teaching Feedback Form		
Student intern name:		School name:
Date of Lesson:	**Subject:**	**Grade Level:**
Day's Lesson Concept:		
Targets	**Cooperating Teacher Feedback**	
Ability to collaborate on the lesson plan with cooperating teacher		
Level of understanding the process of constructing a lesson plan		
Level of planning and preparation for lesson		
Level of understanding of content objectives		
Level of comfort in teacher role		
Ability to maintain eye contact and student's attention		
Ability to effectively sequence the lesson		
Ability to effectively time each activity		
Ability to implement existing instructional strategies and materials to teach lesson		
What suggestions do you have to help your intern improve?		
1.		
2.		
Additional Comments:		

Cooperating teacher signature: _____

Evaluate Your Effectiveness After Teaching a Lesson

Activity F   **Name** _____   **Date** _____   **Period** _____

Complete the following self-evaluation after teaching one or more lessons.

Targets	Student Reflection
Ability to collaborate on the lesson plan with cooperating teacher	
Level of understanding the process of constructing a lesson plan	
Level of planning and preparation for lesson	
Level of understanding of content objectives	
Level of comfort in teacher role	
Ability to maintain eye contact and student's attention	
Ability to effectively sequence the lesson	
Ability to effectively time each activity	
Ability to implement existing instructional strategies and materials to teach lesson	
What three targets would you like most to improve?	**What can you, your cooperating teacher, or your classroom teacher do to help you improve those characteristics?**
1.	
2.	
3.	

After completing this form, meet with your cooperating teacher and discuss your responses and his or her evaluation of your performance. Write additional comments on a separate sheet of paper.

Intern signature _____   **Date** _____

Chapter 13
Technology for Instruction

Building Your Pedagogical Vocabulary

Activity A **Name** _____ **Date** _____ **Period** _____

Define the terms in the following chart and create an *app icon* to represent the term (similar to those you see representing digital content).

Term	Definition	Icon
Instructional technology		
Distance education		
Online learning		
Virtual school		
Interactive whiteboard		
Model		

(Continued)

Term	Definition	Icon
Acceptable use policy		
WebQuest		
Accredited		
Real time		
Plagiarism		
Copyright		
TEACH Act of 2002		
Multimedia		

Evaluating Technology Usage

Name _____   **Date** _____   **Period** _____

Consider the use of technology in your own daily life. Complete the checklist and the questions that follow in the space provided.

Device	Own or Have Access To	Frequency of Use (Check (✓) the box after each device that best fits the number of times you use the device each week.)			
		Less than once a week	Four to six times a week	Daily	Multiple times daily
Computer/laptop					
Smartphone					
Video-game console					
Tablet					
Portable gaming device					

(Continued)

Device	Own or Have Access To	Frequency of Use (Check (✓) the box after each device that best fits the number of times you use the device each week.)			
		Less than once a week	Four to six times a week	Daily	Multiple times daily
Wearable smart technology *(including fitness trackers & clothing technology)*					
Other?					

Tzubasa/Shutterstock.com; sdp_creations/Shutterstock.com; Chesky/Shutterstock.com.

1. Review your answers. Are you surprised by any of your usage patterns? Why or why not?

   _____

   _____

   _____

2. Consider the technology you use on a daily basis. How does this technology enhance your life?

   _____

   _____

   _____

   _____

3. Estimate the amount of time combined you spend using the various forms of technology each day, checking e-mail, texts, social media, gaming, homework, etc.

   _____

   _____

4. Does the amount of time surprise you? Why or why not?

   _____

   _____

   _____

   _____

5. Consider your favorite form of technology and the classroom in which you are an intern. How could you create a lesson to incorporate your favorite technology source into the lesson?

   _____

   _____

   _____

   _____

Adapting Lesson Plans Using Technology

Activity C   **Name** _____   **Date** _____   **Period** _____

More and more, teachers are looking for ways to transform paper-based lessons and activities to those that are technology-based. Here is an example showing how to transform a totally paper-based lesson to a technology-based lesson.

> *When teaching a lesson on healthy choices in a health or nutrition class, a teacher might have students circle their healthiest choices on a worksheet after the lesson. To incorporate the new interactive whiteboard, you design a lesson that allows students to come up one at a time and choose the healthiest option using an interactive program. Students continue to use the worksheet to follow along and record their answers, and the paper copy serves as a backup in case there is a technology glitch.*

Part 1: Ask your cooperating teacher for a short lesson that he or she would like to convert to a technology-based lesson. Review the lesson with your teacher and take notes in the space provided. Complete online research for technology options to enhance the lesson and create a rough draft of the new lesson plan in the space provided. Review it with your cooperating teacher before typing up a final copy (refer to previously learned lesson plan details).

1. What are the objectives or learning outcomes for the students? (Use words from Bloom's Taxonomy to complete the statement.)

    The students will be able to _____

    _____

    _____

    _____

2. How can technology enhance this lesson? _____

    _____

    _____

    _____

3. What technology is available to use in your cooperating classroom? _____

    _____

4. Do you need any special permission to access this type of software/technology (is it school approved)?

    _____

5. Do the students have enough prior knowledge for using the technology appropriately, or will they need instruction on the technology or software use chosen prior to the lesson? Explain.

    _____

    _____

    _____

6. Will any accommodations need to be made for specific students? _____

    _____

7. How can you assess the value of the learning experience? _____

    _____

(Continued)

ROUGH DRAFT Lesson Plan	Subject:	Grade Level:
General Unit of Study	Name of unit:	
Day's Lesson Concept/Topic	Name of lesson concept or topic:	
Specific Objectives	*Students will be able to* • _____ _____ • _____ _____ How will you link the new materials to prior learning? _____ _____	
Introduction (Hook)	How will you engage the students right away? _____ _____	
Step-by-Step Procedures (Details including instructional strategies you will use and timing.) • Introduction/transitions • Teacher talking • Student interactions • Individual/group work • Activity	_____ _____ _____ _____ _____	
Summary (Closure)	How will you summarize and check for understanding?	
Assessment	How will you assess student growth and learning?	
Instructional Materials and Equipment	What materials will you use to teach the lesson?	
Adaptations for Students Who Have Special Needs		
Learning Styles to Address	How are you addressing all three learning styles in this lesson?	
Notes		

Part 2: Observe your cooperating teacher deliver the technology-enhanced lesson or deliver it yourself! Then reflect on the potential effectiveness of the technology-integrated lesson versus the traditionally taught lesson.

Investigating Virtual Schools

Activity D   **Name** _____   **Date** _____   **Period** _____

With hundreds of virtual schools in the United States educating over 250,000 students, it is important to understand the options available to students and the qualifications of the education they offer.

Part 1: Search online for information regarding virtual schools in your state, using the questions that follow to guide your inquiry. Write your responses in the space provided.

1. What is the status of virtual schools in your state? Are they public? private? Explain.

_____

_____

_____

_____

Part 2: Choose one school on which to focus on that provides online education in your state. List its name and website and then answer the questions that follow about the school.

Name of virtual school: _____

Website of virtual school: _____

2. What is this school's student-to-teacher ratio? In what ways can this impact the students' experience?

_____

_____

_____

_____

_____

3. What courses are offered?

_____

_____

_____

_____

_____

4. How are courses delivered? Are they delivered only online, or is blended learning utilized?

_____

_____

_____

_____

5. How does a teacher work with the students if they have questions on a lesson?

_____

_____

_____

(Continued)

6. How are parents involved in the education of their children? _____

_____

_____

_____

_____

7. In what ways does the school assist students who struggle (*Response to Intervention* or *Special Education*)?

_____

_____

_____

_____

8. Does the school offer educational opportunities for multiple levels of students? Explain.

_____

_____

_____

_____

9. Summarize how the courses and requirements are aligned with state standards.

_____

_____

_____

_____

_____

10. Does the school provide opportunities for curriculum enhancement through field trips or guest speakers? Explain.

_____

_____

_____

_____

_____

Part 3: After completing your responses, expand your knowledge of virtual schools by doing one of the following.

A. Compile a paper focusing on one virtual school. Share your findings with the class using a school-approved form of presentation technology.

B. Compare and contrast the school you researched to those researched by one of your peers. Describe how the schools are similar and different.

C. Compare the virtual school to your current school. What are the benefits and drawbacks of each? Discuss your findings with the class.

Assistive Technology in Use

Activity E   **Name** _____   **Date** _____   **Period** _____

Consider the use of assistive technology in your school or the school in which you are interning. Interview a paraprofessional, administrator, or teacher who works with a student using some form of assistive technology. Write the responses from your interview in the space provided.

Name of professional: _____

Number of students using assistive technology: _____

Signature of professional acknowledging contact: _____

1. What type(s) of assistive technology is (are) used by students in the school?

   _____

   _____

   _____

   _____

   _____

   _____

2. How does use of assistive technology impact student learning? _____

   _____

   _____

   _____

   _____

   _____

   _____

   _____

   _____

   _____

3. Who purchases and supports the technology? How frequently is it updated? _____

   _____

   _____

   _____

   _____

4. How are students and teachers trained to use assistive technologies? _____

   _____

   _____

   _____

   _____

(Continued)

5. What are some challenges that you have had to overcome with use of assistive technology?

_____

_____

_____

_____

_____

_____

_____

6. Are students able to use the technology outside of the school day? at home? during sports? or when participating in activities as a spectator?

_____

_____

_____

_____

_____

_____

_____

7. When a student leaves this school or transitions to another school, does the assistive technology travel with the student, or how is a transition supported?

_____

_____

_____

_____

_____

_____

_____

8. What are some additional observations about the use of assistive technology in the classroom?

_____

_____

_____

_____

_____

_____

_____

Creating a Podcast

Activity F   **Name** _____ **Date** _____ **Period** _____

A podcast can be created to meet one of the following criteria as determined by your cooperating teacher. The following ideas are suggestions that are meant to help you brainstorm creative ways to use the technology to enhance student learning. Every student can benefit from these.

- To assist all students in reviewing material
  a. Create a song that reviews the information in a catchy way
  b. Have the students read the material and record them, then put together in your podcast
- To individualize the learning for a student who has special needs
  a. Provide wait time after information is given in podcast
  b. Align podcast with worksheet and allow student to respond to prompts in podcast
- To allow access to a student whose primary language is not English
  a. Create a bilingual podcast for all students to learn from
- To provide a more in-depth learning opportunity for advanced students
  a. Provide information that allows advanced students to think about content in a different way
  b. Prompt students to associate content with current events

Part 1: Review the following steps for creating a podcast.

1. Identify the objective and main points of the lesson
2. Compose a script of the audio you will read for the podcast
3. Research audio clips to enhance the lesson (must be public domain and copyright free); use a minimum of two audio clips
4. Save audio clips or links
5. Practice the script (you will be reading), record it, and then listen to it
6. Set up equipment (Do you need anything for added sound effects?)
7. Record the podcast in short segments, aim for 3–5 minutes
8. Save frequently as you record
9. After recording everything, edit your podcast using school-approved editing software (save your original files as a backup first)!
10. Splice together your recorded content and music or sound effects
11. Review the podcast
12. Publish or share the final piece with the class

Part 2: Use the following prompts to plan your podcast. If necessary, use additional sheets of paper for planning and writing your script and attach them to this activity sheet.

1. The students will be able to _____

_____

_____

(Continued)

2. Main points to address _____

_____

_____

_____

_____

_____

3. List potential sources for audio clips to enhance the lesson (must be public domain and copyright free); use a minimum of two audio clips.

_____

_____

_____

_____

4. Is there a benefit to incorporating students into the recording? Explain _____

_____

_____

5. What additional sounds, music, etc., might enhance the audio? _____

_____

6. What equipment will you need and how can you access it? _____

_____

_____

7. Do you need to create any supplemental material for students to use with the podcast? Explain.

_____

_____

8. When would your cooperating teacher like the podcast finished for his or her review prior to sharing with the class or student(s)?

_____

_____

9. How can you publish the file to share with students? _____

_____

_____

10. Will students be able to download it to their own devices? _____

11. Would it be appropriate or beneficial to share the podcast with the parents or community? Explain.

_____

_____

Part 3: Create your podcast containing the script and information from your plan with information from a lesson your cooperating teacher will be teaching. You will need a recording device (some cell phones can do this), Internet access, a device on which to save all your content, and an editing app or software (school-approved; available online). (*Note*: Check with the technology coordinator at your school or search online for a tutorial if you are unfamiliar with how to assemble a podcast.)

Virtual Field Trip or Simulated Experience

Activity G   **Name** _____   **Date** _____   **Period** _____

Field trips create opportunities for students to connect the classroom content to the community outside of the school. Sometimes it is one of the most memorable student experiences, igniting interest and a drive to learn! Field trips can be expensive and time-consuming; technology allows the opportunities for exposure to experiences outside the classroom to increase without the expense!

Your task is to create a virtual field trip or simulated experience for the classroom in which you are interning. Your cooperating teacher may or may not choose to use the experience you create, but the value for you as an aspiring educator is in the planning process. When you have completed all your research, compile your field-trip or simulated-experience planning guide into a typed document and save a printed or digital copy. This will also provide an excellent artifact to include in your portfolio.

Use the following outline as a guide to gather information.

1. **Purpose.** What unit of study is coming up that could benefit from a field trip or simulated experience? Brainstorm at least five ideas in the following space.

   _____

   _____

   _____

   _____

2. **Field-trip destination.** Search online, ask other teachers, and record your ideas. You could even create your own digital field trip content!

   _____

   _____

   _____

   _____

3. **Reservation process.** Will you need to contact anyone at the site or is the entire content available online? Explain. If needed list names, phone numbers, or e-mail addresses of those who can assist you with setting up the simulated experience or field trip.

   _____

   _____

   _____

   _____

   _____

4. **Fees.** Is there a charge to access the technology? Explain. For instance some virtual field trips charge an access fee. How would you pay this? Is there a school budget for this type of experience? Ask your cooperating teacher or principal about this.

   _____

   _____

   _____

   _____

(Continued)

5. **Notify parents/guardians.** How do parents know about the upcoming trip—is there a class newsletter, a special note sent home, an online site or social media feed? Create a notice to parents/guardians containing the pertinent information about the field trip or simulated experience, including what, when, where, and what fees may be involved. Make sure you explain the benefits of the experience and how the students will be participating individually or as a class. Write the draft or your notice in the space that follows.

_____

_____

_____

_____

_____

_____

_____

6. **Permissions.** Does the school require a permission form from parents/guardians to allow students to access information on the web? Many schools have a form parents or guardians sign when they enroll their children that allows them to access content on the Internet. Ask to see if this form exists or if you should create one for your activity. Attach a copy to this activity sheet.

7. **Technology access.** Will students be accessing the virtual field trip or simulated experience as homework on their own? Will you be projecting it on a screen? Will students need headsets? These and other considerations will determine what technology you need to have available for this experience. Work with your schools technology or media coordinator or your cooperating teacher to reserve the equipment. Document what equipment you need and how you arranged for the access ahead of time in the following space.

_____

_____

_____

_____

_____

8. **Leading questions.** Create at least five leading questions to guide students further into the content of the experience.

_____

_____

_____

_____

_____

9. Type up all of the information you have collected from this project, including each of the prompts above. Anyone should be able to take your project and recreate the experience for their students.

10. If you are able to share this experience with your class, write a summary about the students' responses to the experience and reflect on the value added to the curricular content. Attach your summary to this activity sheet.

11. Use the rubric in *Activity H* for self-assessment and cooperating teacher assessment.

Self-Assessment: Virtual Field Trip or Simulated Experience

Activity H   **Name** _____ **Date** _____ **Period** _____

Part 1. Complete the following self-assessment related to planning and executing a virtual field trip or simulated experience. Write your comments in the space provided.

Self-Assessment for Virtual Experiences		
Project Parts	**Points Possible**	**Comments**
Purpose (Clear and relevant to the class.)	15	
Destination (The experience aligns to goals and objectives.)	5	
Reservation process (Explain if required.)	5	
Fees and funding (Explain fee determination even if not required.)	5	
Parent notification (Effectively created.)	10	
Permissions (How are students/parents/guardians consenting to web-based access?)	5	
Technology (How did you arrange for needed technology? What was needed?)	5	
Questioning (Evaluate the effectiveness of questions asked throughout the experience.)	15	
Final presentation (All points above have been formally addressed. Presentation enables other teachers to arrange the same experience for their students is professional, neat, has no grammatical errors, and is portfolio ready.)	25	
Self-reflection (Evaluate your performance on the assignment and what you learned.)	10	
Additional student comments:		
Total points possible: 100	**Total points earned:**	

Student intern signature _____ **Date** _____

Part 2. Have your cooperating teacher complete the following rubric to evaluate your virtual experiences project.

Cooperating Teacher Assessment for Virtual Experiences		
Project Parts	Points Possible	Comments
Purpose (Clear and relevant to the class.)	15	
Destination (The experience objectives effectively align to curricular goals.)	5	
Reservation process (Explained if required.)	5	
Fees and funding (Appropriate explanation provided.)	5	
Parent notification (Effectively created.)	10	
Permissions (How were students/parents/guardians consenting to web-based access?)	5	
Technology (Identified needs. Arrangements for needed technology made properly?)	5	
Questioning (Evaluate the effectiveness of questions asked throughout the experience.)	15	
Final presentation (All points above have been addressed in a formal format. Presentation enables other teachers to arrange the same experience for their students. The presentation is professional, neat, has no grammatical errors, and is portfolio ready.)	25	
Self-reflection (Evaluate student performance on the assignment and what was learned.)	10	
Additional teacher comments:		
Total points possible:100	Total points earned:	

Cooperating teacher signature _____ Date_____

Determining Acceptable Use and Internet Safety

Activity I   **Name** _____   **Date** _____   **Period** _____

Part 1: Conduct research on your school, or the school in which you intern, regarding the use of the Internet at school and during school hours. Determine the school's acceptable use policy. Use the following questions to guide your research. Write your responses in the space provided.

1. Does the school mandate Internet safety curriculum? Explain why or why not. Some states require Internet safety to be taught before students access the Internet. Does your school teach it, and if so, how?

_____

_____

_____

_____

_____

2. Does the school have an acceptable use of technology policy? If so, briefly summarize it. Is this policy different for students and staff? How is it communicated to students and staff?

_____

_____

_____

_____

_____

3. What are the expectations for network etiquette *(netiquette)*? How are these expectations communicated to students and staff?

_____

_____

_____

_____

_____

4. What is the school's stated intended use of the Internet? If no policy exists, write an intended use statement.

_____

_____

_____

_____

_____

_____

(Continued)

5. When can privileges for using the Internet be revoked? What security risks are addressed with students and staff? If no policy exists, draft a statement regarding security and revocation of Internet privileges.

_____

_____

_____

_____

_____

_____

_____

_____

_____

6. How does the school filter and block inappropriate sites? The *Child and Internet Protection Act (CIPA)* requires schools to protect children from inappropriate content. What is the process to report something inappropriate and to unblock sites that you may need for class use?

_____

_____

_____

_____

_____

_____

_____

_____

_____

_____

Part 2: Share your findings with the class. Compare and contrast different schools' policies, documentation, and how the policies are communicated to families, students, and staff. Record notes or questions that arise from this discussion in the following space.

_____

_____

_____

_____

_____

_____

_____

_____

_____

_____

_____

_____

_____

Copyright and Fair Use in Education

Activity J   Name _____ Date _____ Period _____

Teachers routinely use news stories, digital media, and published sources as information to share in the classroom. Laws are changing frequently, however, and an effective reference guide would be a great resource for keeping track of copyright laws and fair use.

Part 1: Individually or in small groups, your task is to conduct research, finding and evaluating sources to assemble a *Copyright and Fair Use Guide* at a glance resource. Use the prompts that follow to begin your research. Then assemble a guide to inform teachers and staff about what the laws say concerning what *can* or *cannot* be used in the classroom. Your final project could be digital or could be in the form of a printed brochure, checklist, or poster.

1. Think of a time a teacher or other speaker may have presented material that was copyrighted. Without using identifying information, describe the situation.

   _____

   _____

   _____

   _____

2. What does the *TEACH Act of 2002* specify regarding use of copyrighted material in schools?

   _____

   _____

   _____

   _____

   _____

   _____

   _____

3. How does the *Copyright Act of 1976* play a role in materials used in schools?

   _____

   _____

   _____

   _____

   _____

   _____

   _____

4. *Fair Use* is a limitation of exception to copyright law. Write a summary identifying what is considered Fair Use.

   _____

   _____

   _____

   _____

(Continued)

5. Refer back to the incident you described in question 1. Knowing what you do now, how does copyright play a role in such presentations of information? Does the *TEACH Act of 2002* provide permission for the work to be used in the classroom? Explain.

_____

_____

_____

_____

_____

_____

6. What sort of reference would help teachers make sure they are not infringing on copyright laws?

_____

7. Briefly summarize how you intend to present your reference information. _____

_____

_____

_____

_____

Part 2: Create a sketch of the basic layout of your reference piece in the following space. What graphics would help represent your information? What information will be the most important for teachers?

Chapter 14
The Role of Assessment

Understanding Assessment Terms

Activity A Name _____ Date _____ Period _____

Use the word bank that follows to match each term to the correct definition. Write the letter of the correct term in the space provided to the left of each number. Then write an example describing when you were exposed to or used this form of assessment.

Terms

A. Alternative assessment
B. Checklist
C. Course evaluation
D. Formative assessment

E. Peer evaluation
F. Rubric
G. Scorecard
H. Self-evaluation

I. Student portfolio
J. Summative assessment

Definitions

_____ 1. As an ongoing part of instruction, a teacher asks students questions about a concept during a lesson which provides feedback about student learning as it occurs.

Example of a time I used this type of assessment: _____

_____

_____

_____

_____ 2. This type of assessment describes levels of quality for judging a particular type of work.

Example of a time I used this type of assessment: _____

_____

_____

_____

_____ 3. A form of assessment that includes a simple list of items to note, check, or remember when students or teachers evaluate learning.

Example of a time I used this type of assessment: _____

_____

_____

_____

_____ 4. A form of assessment that lists the factors to evaluate and offers the maximum point value.

Example of a time I used this type of assessment: _____

_____

_____

_____

(Continued)

Terms

A. Alternative assessment
B. Checklist
C. Course evaluation
D. Formative assessment

E. Peer evaluation
F. Rubric
G. Scorecard
H. Self-evaluation

I. Student portfolio
J. Summative assessment

Definitions (continued)

_____ 5. A form assessment administered after instruction has taken place.

Example of a time I used this type of assessment: _____

_____

_____

_____

_____ 6. A form of assessment that allows students to gauge their own understanding.

Example of a time I used this type of assessment: _____

_____

_____

_____

_____ 7. A collection of a student's work that shows growth and development, and highlights skills and achievements over time.

Example of a time I used this type of assessment: _____

_____

_____

_____

_____ 8. A type of assessment that judges how well a course meets its goals and what improvements would make it better.

Example of a time I used this type of assessment: _____

_____

_____

_____

_____ 9. A form of assessment through which a student's peers judge whether criteria was met.

Example of a time I used this type of assessment: _____

_____

_____

_____

_____ 10. A form of assessment that encourages creativity and real-life application.

Example of a time I used this type of assessment: _____

_____

_____

_____

Creating and Evaluating Test Questions

Activity B   **Name** _____ **Date** _____ **Period** _____

Part 1: The following provides a curriculum standard to use for writing test questions. Write two examples of each type of question that could be used to demonstrate competency of this third-grade standard. Use the fairy tale *Cinderella* or another story your teacher assigns. Remember to refer to Bloom's Taxonomy to challenge students to reach multiple levels of comprehension. Review your test questions before proceeding to *Part 2*.

English Language Arts Literacy Standard—Grade 3: Describe the characters in a story (for example, their traits, motivations, or feelings) and explain how their actions contribute to the sequence of events.

True-false Questions

1. _____

_____

_____

2. _____

_____

_____

Multiple-choice Questions

1. _____

_____

_____

   A. _____
   B. _____
   C. _____
   D. _____

2. _____

_____

_____

   A. _____
   B. _____
   C. _____
   D. _____

Matching Questions

1. _____

_____

_____

(Continued)

2. _____

_____

_____

_____

Options for matching questions:

A. _____

_____

B. _____

_____

Fill-in-the-blank Questions

1. _____

_____

_____

2. _____

_____

_____

Identification Questions (Use the space to the right to draw your diagram)

1. _____

_____

_____

_____

2. _____

_____

_____

_____

Essay Questions

1. _____

_____

_____

_____

_____

2. _____

_____

_____

_____

_____

(Continued)

Name _____

Part 2: Create an answer key for the test questions you created above and reflect on the questions you wrote.

True-false Questions

1. _____
   _____

2. _____
   _____

Multiple-choice Questions

1. _____

2. _____

Matching Questions

1. _____

2. _____

Fill-in-the-blank Questions

1. _____

2. _____

Identification Questions (Use the space to the right to draw your diagram)

1. _____
   _____
   _____
   _____

2. _____
   _____
   _____
   _____

Essay Questions

1. _____
   _____
   _____
   _____
   _____
   _____

2. _____
   _____
   _____
   _____
   _____
   _____

(Continued)

Part 3: Evaluate your test questions and answers by completing the following questions. Write your responses in the space provided.

1. Did you write questions that used multiple levels of comprehension? Explain and give an example of how you achieved this.

   _____
   _____
   _____
   _____
   _____
   _____

2. Explain why it is important to write questions to multiple levels. _____

   _____
   _____
   _____
   _____
   _____
   _____

3. How did your questions demonstrate comprehension of the *English Language Arts Literacy Standard—Grade 3: Describe characters in a story (e.g., their traits, motivations, or feelings) and explain how their actions contribute to the sequence of events?* Explain in detail how your questions met this standard.

   _____
   _____
   _____
   _____
   _____
   _____

4. Consider the questions you created. Which type(s) of question do you think would help a student with limited English proficiency demonstrate his or her comprehension and why?

   _____
   _____
   _____
   _____
   _____
   _____

Standardized Testing and Its Role in Education

Activity C **Name** _____ **Date** _____ **Period** _____

Consider all the standardized tests you have taken as a student. Conduct research regarding standardized tests by your high school or the school at which you are an intern. In many states, this information can be found on the *School Report Card*. In other states, you might need to interview an administrator to answer the questions that follow.

1. Source of information: _____

2. Describe how well students in this school are performing on standardized tests. Give percentages meeting or exceeding standards.

   _____

   _____

   _____

   _____

   _____

   _____

3. Evaluate student scores over time. What trends do your observe in the data? Is there anything that happened to support these trends? You may need to dig deeper to substantiate your analysis.

   _____

   _____

   _____

   _____

   _____

   _____

4. Compare and contrast the scores of students in categories such as special education, low income, or ethnically diverse to the standardized score for the school/grade. What are the similarities and differences?

   _____

   _____

   _____

   _____

   _____

   _____

5. Generate two additional questions you have regarding standardized test scores as reported for students.

   a. _____

   _____

   b. _____

   _____

(Continued)

6. What information, if any, is provided regarding student attendance? If provided, can you cross-reference the information with test scores as reported? Explain.

_____

_____

_____

_____

_____

7. What does this report tell you about the teachers in the district and their expertise?

_____

_____

_____

8. What information regarding the amount of money spent per pupil in the school is provided?

_____

_____

9. What correlations can you make regarding spending per pupil and test scores?

_____

_____

_____

_____

_____

10. Record any additional information you found in the report card. _____

_____

_____

_____

_____

_____

11. If one of your peers focused on a different school, compare the findings. Then list several items of interest from your analysis.

_____

_____

_____

_____

_____

Positive Reinforcement, A–Z

Activity D   **Name** _____   **Date** _____   **Period** _____

Part 1: Focused, positive feedback is important for teachers to use during and following instruction. For each letter of the alphabet that follows, come up with one positive, affirming word. Then write a sentence demonstrating how to use the term as focused feedback. It is important to vary your positive statements during teaching; this exercise will give you some great ideas! An example has been provided.

A. **Amazing.** *"Jenny, you did an amazing job identifying the food groups on MyPlate."*

B. _____

_____

C. _____

_____

D. _____

_____

E. _____

_____

F. _____

_____

G. _____

_____

H. _____

_____

I. _____

_____

J. _____

_____

K. _____

_____

L. _____

_____

M. _____

_____

N. _____

_____

O. _____

_____

(Continued)

P. _____

_____

Q. _____

_____

R. _____

_____

S. _____

_____

T. _____

_____

U. _____

_____

V. _____

_____

W. _____

_____

X. _____

_____

Y. _____

_____

Z. _____

_____

Part 2: Recreate the list in a decorative poster format and keep it by your desk when grading and writing lesson plans. In the space that follows, create a quick sketch of what your poster may look like.

Creating a Rubric

Activity E   **Name** _____   **Date** _____   **Period** _____

Part 1: Collaborate with your cooperating teacher to design a rubric that allows for self-assessment by the students as well as assist the teacher in grading a project. Refer back to the rubrics provided for you to self-assess in the previous chapters. Remember that some grade levels and projects might require actual point values while others might simply use pictures or symbols representing developing content. Review the expectations with your teacher prior to creating a rough draft of the rubric. Make sure you provide a digital copy of the rubric to your cooperating teacher for future use. Remember, rubrics take time to develop and, after they are used once, they need to be reevaluated for effectiveness.

1. Name the project/activity to be evaluated with the rubric. _____
   _____

2. Based on the level of the students, will they relate best to points, pictures, or text in the rubric?
   _____

3. How many columns do you want to include? three options? four options? (Sometimes providing an even number of options is best so that students do not always pick the average or middle value.)
   _____

4. How would you describe the highest level of achievement? _____
   _____
   _____
   _____
   _____

5. How would you describe the level that provides for the greatest amount of improvement? _____
   _____
   _____
   _____
   _____

6. What criteria will the rubric assess (rows)? _____
   _____
   _____
   _____
   _____

Part 2: Create a rough draft of the rubric using the template on page 146. Review the rubric with your cooperating teacher before typing it up and turning in the final copy. *Optional:* Ask your cooperating teacher if he or she could use the rubric in class and provide you with feedback on its success. If possible, observe the use of your rubric. Reflect on your observation and make any changes needed in the rubric to increase effectiveness.

(Continued)

Rough Draft Rubric

(*Note*: Cross out any boxes that are not needed.)

Chapter 15
Classroom Management

Building Your Pedagogical Vocabulary

Activity A   Name _____   Date _____   Period _____

Part 1: Define the terms that follow as you read Chapter 15. Write your definitions in the space provided.

Term	Definition
Classroom management	
Authoritarian style	
Permissive style	
Authoritative style	
School policies	
Class rules	
Classroom procedures	
Nonverbal cues	
Perseverance	
Insubordination	

(Continued)

Part 2: Compose a short, school-appropriate story that demonstrates the proper use of the chapter terms in an educational setting. Write your story in the space that follows. If necessary, use an additional sheet of paper to complete your story and attach it to this activity sheet.

_____

_____

_____

_____

_____

_____

_____

_____

_____

_____

_____

_____

_____

_____

_____

_____

_____

_____

_____

_____

_____

_____

Part 3: After writing your school-appropriate story, write three assessment questions (with answers) about your story in the space that follows. Then share your story with the class. Ask the class your review questions to assess how well your classmates have learned the terms.

1. Question: _____

   _____

   Answer: _____

   _____

2. Question: _____

   _____

   Answer: _____

   _____

3. Question: _____

   _____

   Answer: _____

   _____

Classroom Layout Analysis

Activity B   **Name** _____ **Date** _____ **Period** _____

Part 1: In the classroom in which you are serving as an intern or cadet, consider the layout. Sketch the current layout in the space that follows. Be sure to label all classroom components and areas including desks, work centers, procedural spaces, whiteboard, computer centers, etc. Then respond to the questions that follow your sketch.

Current Classroom Layout

```




```

1. List at least three things you would change about this layout environment for your own classroom.

_____

_____

_____

2. Why would you want to make these changes? _____

_____

_____

_____

(Continued)

Part 2: In the space that follows, sketch an alternative layout that you would like to try. Keep in mind the classroom management tips provided by the text. Be sure to label all classroom components and areas. Then respond to the questions that follow your sketch.

Proposed Classroom Layout

1. Describe in detail the specific changes you made in the classroom layout environment. _____

_____

_____

_____

_____

2. Cite at least three text statements that support the changes you are suggesting for the classroom layout environment.

_____

_____

_____

_____

Student Engagement Lesson Plan

Activity C   **Name** _____   **Date** _____   **Period** _____

Part 1: Work with your cooperating teacher to identify with a lesson you can modify to increase student engagement. Use the following space to prepare and to write the lesson plan and teach the lesson (*optional*).

1. Ask the teacher to describe how he or she would teach the lesson. What instructional strategies does the teacher typically use?

   _____

2. Does he or she want the lesson format to stay the same or is there some flexibility? Explain.

   _____

3. What characteristics about this lesson make your cooperating teacher want it revised to increase student engagement?

   _____

4. What resources are available to help to prepare you for the lesson?_____

   _____

5. How will you assess learning? _____

   _____

6. How long does the lesson need to be? When will you teach it?

   _____

7. What prior knowledge will students have obtained from previous lessons? What knowledge will they need to be successful with the following lesson?

   _____

8. What accommodations or modifications need to be made for specific students?

   _____

9. In thinking about this lesson, brainstorm some initial thoughts on ways you can increase engagement and discuss their feasibility with your cooperating teacher.

   _____

Part 2: Using the information you have gathered and text details, create a lesson plan following the format provided. Once you complete the following form, type up your lesson and ask your cooperating teacher to review it and approve it. Make revisions as your cooperating teacher suggests.

Lesson Plan		
Intern Name: _____		
School: _____		
Co-op teacher approval signature _____		
Date of Lesson:	**Subject:**	**Grade Level:**
General Unit of Study	Name of unit:	
Day's Lesson Concept/Topic	Name of lesson concept or topic:	

(Continued)

Lesson Plan

Learner Characteristics	Number of students: Age(s): Boys: Girls: Special needs: Behavior issues:
Specific Objectives What are two or three main things you want students to learn from your lesson? Written objectives should be **measurable** and follow Bloom's taxonomy. Use the phrase, "Students will be able to" and then begin the objective with verb from Bloom's Taxonomy followed by objective.	*Students will be able to* • _____ _____ • _____ _____ • _____ _____ • _____ _____ How will you link the new materials to prior learning? _____ _____
Time Period	
Introduction (Hook)	How will you engage the students right away? _____ _____
Step-by-Step Procedures (Details including instructional strategies you will use and timing**.)** • Introduction/transitions • Teacher talking • Questioning • Student interactions • Individual seat work • Small group work • Activity • Lesson closure	_____ _____ _____ _____ _____ _____ _____ _____ _____ _____ _____

(Continued)

Name _____

Lesson Plan	
Summary (Closure)	How will you summarize and check for understanding? _____ _____
Assessment	How will you assess student growth and learning? _____ _____
Instructional Materials and Equipment	What materials will you use to teach the lesson? _____ _____
Adaptations for Students Who Have Special Needs	_____ _____
Learning Styles to Address	How are you addressing all three learning styles in this lesson? _____ _____
Notes	_____ _____ _____

Cooperating teacher signature (approval): _____ **Date** _____

Part 3. Use the items that follow to summarize the outcomes of the revisions you made to the unit to increase student engagement.

10. Specifically detail changes you implemented in the lesson to increase student engagement in this lesson.

_____

_____

11. If you are able to observe or interview the teacher after the lesson is taught, or you are able to teach it, discuss the outcome of the revisions. How did your revisions to the lesson increase student engagement?

_____

_____

12. If your lesson changes did *not* increase student engagement, identify several possible reasons why these changes had little impact.

_____

_____

13. Did additional concerns arise as a result of the changes to the lesson? If so, elaborate on these concerns.

_____

_____

14. What suggestions do you have for further revisions to the lesson to deal with these additional concerns? Cite text references to support your revision suggestions.

_____

_____

Creating Start-Up Assignments

Activity D   **Name** _____   **Date** _____   **Period** _____

Many lessons start with a period of transition from one activity to the next. Start-up activity time can allow the students to engage in learning while the teacher works to transition individual students. Working with your cooperating teacher, choose a unit that could benefit from start-up prompts. Create at least five prompts for the entire unit and provide them to your cooperating teacher for use. Save a copy for future use in your portfolio.

1. In detail for the identified lesson unit, write the objectives for the start-up activities you will create.

   a. _____

   b. _____

   c. _____

   d. _____

   e. _____

2. In what format will the prompts be communicated to students (projected, written on board, journal prompt, etc.)?

   _____

   _____

   _____

3. How will students respond to the start-ups (worksheet, journal, small-group discussion, etc.)?

   _____

   _____

   _____

4. Briefly describe your five prompts in the space that follows.

   a. _____

   b. _____

   c. _____

   d. _____

   e. _____

5. Explain how you will provide the prompts to your cooperating teacher for ease of use. For example, you might provide each prompt on one slide in a digital presentation format to be projected each day.

   _____

   _____

   _____

   _____

   _____

   _____

   _____

   _____

   _____

Analyzing Reward Systems

Activity E   **Name** _____   **Date** _____   **Period** _____

Reward systems can play a vital role in classroom management. Observe the reward system used within the classroom in which you are serving as a teacher intern or cadet. *(If no reward system is used, seek out another classroom that uses a reward system.)* In the space provided, explain the rewards the teacher uses and analyze their effectiveness. Share your findings with fellow interns or cadets.

1. Explain the reward system in use in your cooperating classroom. _____
   _____
   _____
   _____
   _____

2. What behaviors are rewarded? _____
   _____
   _____
   _____
   _____

3. How are expectations for behavior communicated to the students? _____
   _____
   _____
   _____
   _____

4. What tangible rewards are associated with the system, if any? _____
   _____
   _____
   _____
   _____

5. What problems have arisen using this reward system? _____
   _____
   _____
   _____
   _____

6. What evidence shows this is an effective system? _____
   _____
   _____
   _____

7. If applicable, take a photograph of the reward system in action and attach it to this activity sheet.

Effective Strategies Scenario

Activity F　　**Name** _____　**Date** _____　**Period** _____

Read the following scenario and then answer the questions that follow. Write your responses in the space provided.

> Mr. Phillips spends the first 15 minutes of class presenting a new topic. After his introduction, the students each choose one of three options to apply the lesson and expand their comprehension of the topic. Mr. Phillips monitors the students and works individually to help the students during the remainder of the class period. During the lesson, Adrienne is using her phone in her lap and occasionally looks up. While the rest of the class is working on their varying assignments, she doesn't even open her notebook. Mr. Phillips asks her which option she is choosing to do. Adrienne doesn't even look up from her phone, and ignores him completely. When he asks her again how he can assist her with the lesson, Adrienne replies "I'm not doing it."

1. What positive teaching strategy did Mr. Phillips use to try and engage Adrienne?

   _____

   _____

   _____

2. What classroom-management policies or procedures could be in place to help avoid this situation?

   _____

   _____

   _____

3. How are Adrienne's actions inappropriate for the learning environment? _____

   _____

   _____

   _____

4. Rewrite the scenario with Mr. Phillips responding to the situation in an effective manner.

   _____

   _____

   _____

   _____

   _____

   _____

   _____

   _____

   _____

   _____

   _____

   _____

Chapter 16
The Next Steps to Becoming a Teacher

Writing a Résumé

Activity A   **Name** _____   **Date** _____   **Period** _____

Part 1: Review the text information for preparing a résumé. Then use the template that follows to begin assembling the information you need for your résumé. Once you have gathered all the information, you will be ready to transfer your résumé to a digital document format.

Your full name: _____

Home phone number: _____   Cell phone number: _____

Your complete address: _____

_____

_____

Appropriate e-mail address:_____

OBJECTIVE(s) (What are your goals for your career? Teaching or otherwise.)

_____

_____

_____

_____

_____

EDUCATIONAL BACKGROUND (High school(s), city, state, and dates attended)

_____

_____

_____

_____

_____

WORK EXPERIENCE (Do you have a job that you get paid for? Name the employer and dates of employment.)

_____

_____

_____

_____

_____

(Continued)

VOLUNTEERISM/SERVICE-LEARNING (What causes do you give your time to? In what school-related service-learning projects have you participated?)

_____

_____

_____

_____

_____

HOBBIES/INTERESTS/SKILLS (What do you do for fun? What are you good at? What software and devices do you have ability to use?)

_____

_____

_____

_____

_____

ACCOMPLISHMENTS/AWARDS (What have you been recognized for?)

_____

_____

_____

_____

_____

MEMBERSHIPS/ACTIVITIES (What do you participate in outside of school?)

_____

_____

_____

_____

_____

Part 2: Choose a digital template that reflects your personality and your professionalism (see the _CareerOneStop_ website or other career research websites to locate résumé templates and sample résumés). Transfer the information you have collected to the template, print the document, and review it for accuracy. Make any corrections or changes before printing your final document to share with the class in a gallery walk.

Writing Your Philosophy of Education

Activity B   Name _____   Date _____   Period _____

Part 1: Early in this course you began the process of formulating your own *philosophy of education*. Since then, you have gained experience in the classroom and can apply your experiences to your initial philosophy. Refer back to your initial philosophy of education and then rubric against which it will be evaluated on the next page. Revise your philosophy of teaching to reflect what you have learned about education. Write your rough draft in the space that follows, including philosophy statements covering each area of expectation from the rubric. Once you complete your philosophy, type it up to include in your portfolio.

Desired Outcomes: _____

_____

_____

_____

_____

_____

_____

_____

_____

_____

_____

_____

Teaching Methods: _____

_____

_____

_____

_____

_____

_____

_____

_____

_____

_____

_____

_____

_____

(Continued)

Assessment Methods: _____

_____

_____

_____

_____

_____

_____

_____

_____

_____

Classroom Diversity: _____

_____

_____

_____

_____

_____

_____

_____

_____

_____

_____

Professional Presentation: _____

_____

_____

_____

_____

_____

_____

_____

_____

_____

_____

_____

(Continued)

Name _____

Part 2: Use the following rubric to self-evaluate your revised philosophy of education. Place a check (✓) in the box identifying the level of expectation you believe you met for each row. Then have your classroom teacher complete the teacher evaluation.

Name: _____			
Self-Evaluation Rubric—Philosophy of Education			
Expectations	**Meets or Exceeds (5)**	**Developing Toward (3)**	**Below (1/0)**
Desired Outcomes Describe how you intend to prepare students to succeed. What does success look like?	Outcomes are clear and specific. Multiple levels of outcomes are clearly addressed and thorough.	Outcomes are clear but not detailed. Knowledge level outcomes are addressed, however higher-level outcomes are lacking.	Outcomes are unclear, inadequate, or absent.
Teaching Methods Highlight methods you have used and how they impact student learning. Be specific, utilizing your experiences in the classroom.	Specific teaching methods and the outcome of their use are detailed. Examples provided of the methods in use within the classroom; description of teaching methods justifies why these methods were chosen for students.	General allusion to teaching methods which are used but not specific. Justification for use in the classroom and/or appropriateness for students missing.	Teaching methods are unclear, inadequate, or absent.
Assessment Methods What do you use to determine student comprehension of objectives? How do assessments reflect standards-based priorities?	A diverse example of assessments administered and their effectiveness is described in detail. Appropriateness for the learning environment is described in detail.	Multiple assessments are not detailed or aligned with the learning environment.	Assessments are unclear, inadequate, or absent.
Classroom Diversity Explain the importance of diverse views in your classroom. Emphasize how you relate to students from a variety of backgrounds.	Provides specific examples of diversity in the classroom environment. Includes student scenarios while protecting their privacy.	Diversity in the classroom is addressed but not in detail.	Diversity is not addressed or tied to the students and environment.
Professional Presentation Philosophy reflects effective formatting, ease of reading, and cohesive thought.	No errors in punctuation, spelling, or grammar.	Minimal errors in punctuation, spelling, or grammar.	Significant errors in punctuation, spelling and/or grammar.
Comments:			

(Continued)

Student intern name: _____

Teacher Evaluation Rubric—Philosophy of Education

Expectations	Meets or Exceeds (5)	Developing Toward (3)	Below (1/0)
Desired Outcomes Describe how you intend to prepare students to succeed. What does success look like?	Outcomes are clear and specific. Multiple levels of outcomes are clearly addressed and thorough.	Outcomes are clear but not detailed. Knowledge level outcomes are addressed, however higher-level outcomes are lacking.	Outcomes are unclear, inadequate, or absent.
Teaching Methods Highlight methods you have used and how they impact student learning. Be specific, utilizing your experiences in the classroom.	Specific teaching methods and the outcome of their use are detailed. Examples provided of the methods in use within the classroom; description of teaching methods justifies why these methods were chosen for students.	General allusion to teaching methods which are used but not specific. Justification for use in the classroom and/or appropriateness for students missing.	Teaching methods are unclear, inadequate, or absent.
Assessment Methods What do you use to determine student comprehension of objectives? How do assessments reflect standards-based priorities?	A diverse example of assessments administered and their effectiveness is described in detail. Appropriateness for the learning environment is described in detail.	Multiple assessments are not detailed or aligned with the learning environment.	Assessments are unclear, inadequate, or absent.
Classroom Diversity Explain the importance of diverse views in your classroom. Emphasize how you relate to students from a variety of backgrounds.	Provides specific examples of diversity in the classroom environment. Includes student scenarios while protecting their privacy.	Diversity in the classroom is addressed but not in detail.	Diversity is not addressed or tied to the students and environment.
Professional Presentation Philosophy reflects effective formatting, ease of reading, and cohesive thought.	No errors in punctuation, spelling, or grammar.	Minimal errors in punctuation, spelling, or grammar.	Significant errors in punctuation, spelling and/or grammar.

Comments:

Total possible points = 25	Your score:

Cooperating teacher signature _____ **Date** _____

Creating Your Electronic Portfolio

Activity C   Name _____   Date _____   Period _____

Part 1: Using the school-approved website of your choice, create an *electronic portfolio* of your teaching experience. Use artifacts created throughout the course to demonstrate your knowledge of the role of a professional educator. The following items must be included in your portfolio; however, you may include additional items to supplement your portfolio.

Teaching experience background including:
- Résumé
- Letter of accomplishment (from cooperating teacher if you have asked for one)
- Philosophy of Education
- Documentation of additional experiences that support your pursuit of teaching

Internship class description including:
- Time, grade level and content taught
- Diversity within the classroom
- Statement of your responsibilities

Lesson plans, handouts, and notes including:
- Lesson plans you have created and taught
- Examples of student work with your feedback (no names)
- Reflective commentary on your lesson and teaching
- Cooperating teacher feedback (from lessons or evaluations)
- Guest speaker assignment
- Virtual field trip assignment

Video/audio recordings of classroom lessons (proper permission must be obtained; optional).

Artifacts, including rubrics, review games, mock field trip, etc. (properly prepared and presented)

Description of efforts to improve your teaching (this may be included in one of the above documents)

Summary of evaluations by students (you may need to create one to elicit feedback or record commentary)

Part 2: Complete the following self-assessment rubric to evaluate your portfolio.

Portfolio Rubric			
Contents	**Exceeds Standard** ____ points	**Meets Standard** ____ points	**Below Standard** ____ points
Artifacts	The association between student achievement in the classroom and teacher effectiveness are evident. Portfolio includes: ***Teacher background including:*** Résumé, philosophy of education, documentation of additional teaching experiences	Contains résumé, philosophy of education, lesson plans, reflection, and other artifacts. The reader is left with few questions. Examples of the student's work in the classroom and impact on learning are evident.	Résumé, philosophy of education, lesson plans, reflection, or other artifacts are missing or incomplete, leaving the reader with significant questions regarding portfolio

(Continued)

Portfolio Rubric			
Artifacts, continued	***Internship class description including:*** Time, grade level, and content taught; diversity within the classroom; statement of responsibilities ***Lesson plans, handouts, and notes including:*** • Audio/video recording of lessons (optional) • Cooperating teacher observation record • Artifacts (including guest speaker and virtual field trip assignments) • Description of personal efforts to improve teaching (may be included in one of the above documents) • Summary of evaluations by students	.	
Organization	Electronic portfolio is well organized and easy to follow. Sections are highlighted and the progression is reasonable. All documents are saved and displayed and PDF or another format that cannot be edited. Contact information (address and phone numbers) are not visible.	The electronic portfolio is organized and easy to follow. Sections are highlighted and the progression is reasonable. Some documents are improperly saved and accessible for reformatting; personal information may be visible.	The electronic version of the portfolio is difficult to navigate; some areas are incomplete or sections are missing.
Professional Presentation	No errors in punctuation, spelling, and/or grammar. Work displayed reflects the student's best efforts and contains revisions of initial work.	Minimal errors in punctuation, spelling, and/or grammar. Work displayed reflects the student's best efforts and contains revisions of initial work	Errors in punctuation, spelling, or grammar make it difficult to follow content. Work displayed does not contain revisions of initial work.
Comments:			
Total points possible:		**Score:**	

Researching Colleges and Universities

Activity D   **Name** _____   **Date** _____   **Period** _____

Part 1: Choose a college or university you are interested in attending. Check with your teacher to assure no other classmates have chosen this institution. Research the college or university website and respond to the items that follow.

1. Name of college or university. _____

2. What major are you interested in pursuing here?_____

   _____

3. List potential employment options with the above cited degree. _____

   _____

4. What is the population of the student body? _____

5. Is the campus located in a rural, urban, or suburban area? _____

6. What are the requirements for admission? _____

   _____

   _____

   _____

   _____

   _____

7. What is the application process including fees, etc.? _____

   _____

   _____

   _____

   _____

8. Is the school accredited? _____ If so, by what accrediting body? _____

   _____

9. What courses are required for your degree? Print the program plan if available and attach it to this activity sheet.

   _____

   _____

   _____

   _____

   _____

   _____

10. Are any classes available online or in a blended format? Explain. _____

   _____

   _____

   _____

(Continued)

11. Is academic assistance or tutoring available on campus? _____

12. Is there a cost for academic assistance? If so, what is the cost? _____

_____

13. What job-placement assistance does this college or university offer? _____

_____

_____

_____

14. Use the tuition and costs calculator to determine the yearly cost of attending the university or college full time. Detail the expenses here.

_____

_____

_____

_____

15. Are there any other expenses not included? (meals, lodging, transportation, etc.) List items that are not included.

_____

_____

16. Are students required to live on campus for a certain number of years? If so, how many?

_____

17. Is campus housing available? If so, what type? _____

_____

18. Are campus jobs available? If so, what jobs interest you? _____

_____

19. What clubs or organizations are available to you as a student? _____

_____

20. Are there study abroad opportunities associated with your program? List one or more opportunities. _____

_____

_____

Part 2: Prepare a digital presentation to share your findings with your class. While your peers are presenting, take note of any colleges or universities of interest to you.

_____

_____

_____

_____